CALLING ALL ELK

By
Jim Zumbo

All photos by the author

ISBN: 0-9624025-0-8

Published by:
Jim Zumbo
Box 2390
Cody, WY 82414

Publishing Consultant:

Jeri D. Walton
Outlaw Books Publishing
Box 4466, Bozeman, MT 59772

Table of Contents

Introduction

A disturbing statistic illustrates a basic fact about elk hunting: two of every ten elk hunters takes an elk each year. Another statistic is even more pessimistic: less than two of every 100 hunters takes a six-point bull or better each year.

Those facts, readers, strongly suggest a couple of obvious conclusions — that elk are tough to hunt, and that big bulls are hard to find.

With those discouraging numbers in mind, it becomes immediately apparent that lots of folks go home from their hunting trips without filling their elk tags. What's more, plenty of hunters never SEE an elk on their hunts.

So how do you turn the odds in your favor? Are there ways to join the group of hunters who dine on elk steaks each year?

Absolutely.

Two vital factors are involved in becoming a top-rate elk hunter: understanding elk behavior, and then doing what it takes to locate and get a good shot at an elk. You must learn elk habits, and I don't mean reading a brief article of an elk's life history. I mean really getting into their patterns and comprehending why they do what they do.

Once you've thoroughly investigated every aspect of an elk's behavior pattern, you can then head for the woods with confidence, but that alone won't make you successful. You must be willing to do what it takes to put your knowledge to work. And that, I'm sorry to say, is hard work — lots of it — like working to the bottom of a timbered canyon, and climbing back out again, like taking a strenuous half-day hike to reach the top of a ridge, like walking, climbing, and sliding five or more miles each day on some of the nastiest terrain you've ever hunted.

Now then, suppose you just aren't capable of a physical workout? Maybe you're at an age where it isn't a good idea, or maybe you simply aren't in shape, or your doctor advises against it. Then what?

Take heart, because I'll explain ways that you can hunt to make it easier on yourself. Your chances won't be as good as the hunter who is physically fit, but at least you won't be wasting your time with little or no opportunity to take an elk.

But let's get back to a basic — how do you learn about elk behavior in the first place?

The best way, of course, is to observe elk in their natural state. That option is practically impossible, because no one, except a wildlife biologist who is paid to watch elk, can afford the luxury of time to hang around elk country.

The next best thing is to spend as much time as possible hunting elk — learning from mistakes and trying to figure why elk behave the way they do. That too is impossible for lots of folks because of the time factor. Even if you live in elk country, you seem to never have enough time to really hunt elk as much as you'd like.

The final option is to read magazine articles and books about elk, to watch instructional videos, and to listen to tape cassettes. Plenty of these tools are on the market. Use them, and acquaint yourself as thoroughly as you can about elk and elk country.

This book is my attempt at acquainting you with a vital behavioral characteristic of elk — VOCALIZATION. By understanding the sounds elk make, and by making certain sounds yourself, you can vastly improve your chances of tying your tag to an elusive elk.

All elk are vocal. Bulls, cows and calves make sounds ALL YEAR LONG. Would you believe that cows bugle? Would you believe bulls make cow chirps? They indeed do, and I'll tell you why they do it, when they do it, and I'll tell you how to respond, or to be aggressive and get THEM to respond.

By now you've probably heard of the cow call. If not, you'll be reading about it a great deal in this book. CALLING ALL ELK deals with both bugling and "cow chirping". Cow calling is the most exciting new hunter's option to come along since we learned how to bugle. It offers an additional dimension to hunting — an exceedingly important one that you MUST understand, and use, if you want to be a complete elk hunter.

I was downright intense when I wrote this book. By the time you're done with it, you'll know why, how, where and when elk make sounds. And you'll know why, how, where, and when to imitate elk sounds yourself.

DO NOT BELIEVE that the advice in CALLING ALL ELK is only good if you're hunting during the September-early October bugle season. The information here can be used from the very earliest hunts in August to the very latest hunts in February. Whether you hunt elk in a pristine wilderness or with enormous crowds of people on a public forest, the techniques in this book will work for you.

I've tried to give you every bit of information I've gleaned from 25 years of elk hunting. During those years I've hunted elk in most major mountain ranges, under varying conditions, and using bow, muzzleloader, and rifle.

I had the good fortune of working with elk as a wildlife biologist, and when I became a full-time outdoor writer in 1978 I put my observations to work. I hunt elk in at least four states each year, as well as a number of trips to Canada's elk country. I made lots of mistakes on those hunts, and I've returned home plenty of times with an unpunched elk tag. But I like to feel that each mistake was a learning process. I've had successes, too. And I've learned from them as well.

This book includes experiences I've had when calling elk, using the bugle and cow call, while hunting on my own, with a couple of pals, or with an outfitter. I've tried to pass on to you some of the things I've learned about elk. Some of those things have never been written about before, and some folks might think I'm crazy. But remember that we're still learning about animals and their behavior patterns. We've made more discoveries over the last 10 or 15 years than we have in all the years put together since we've settled this great country.

My first elk book, HUNT ELK, is a 260-page hardcover that details all facets of elk hunting. CALLING ALL ELK is a supplement to that earlier work. This book exclusively addresses the exciting challenges of understanding and mimicking elk.

I hope you learn something from this book. And then, with what you've learned, I hope you use that information when you head for elk country.

Your elk hunts CAN be successful. You can beat the odds. Remember, it takes two things—knowledge, and then following through by putting that knowledge to work.

Go for it. I wish you the best of luck in our magnificent elk woods.

Jim Zumbo
Cody, Wyoming

Chapter 1

Elk Hunting Basics

(NOTE: This chapter describes and capsulizes elk hunting today, addressing some of the old techniques as well as modern methods. You'll note duplication here, but not because I'm getting absent-minded in my old age . . . sometimes we need to read something two or three times before it sinks in. This book is a learning tool — so it's necessary to repeat important aspects. If you read only this chapter, you'll have a very basic idea of modern elk hunting.)

Elk country can be merciless. It is almost always rugged, with lots of uneven, broken terrain, and it's usually a vast, roadless area that requires plenty of hiking, climbing, falling, and cussing.

Elk themselves are just as difficult. Besides living in big country, they themselves are big, requiring a great deal of preparation and muscle to move a 600-pound carcass a few yards or a few miles, whatever the case may be.

Despite their bigness, elk are not easy to find, as countless thousands of hunters have learned during fruitless outings. It's no surprise among veteran hunters that the average hunter success rate in all elk states combined is less than 20 percent.

Obviously, a lot of folks are doing a lot of things wrong.

There are three distinctive elk seasons. Hunters who recognize that basic fact will quickly improve their score. The bugle, transition, and late season make up the fall hunts; each requires different techniques. (A fourth season occurs prior to the bugle season — relatively few archers hunt during the period).

When you think of an elk, you think of a big bugling bull. Here he is, standing guard over his harem.

Those techniques vary considerably, with many new developments over the last few years. Modern hunters are learning more about animal behavior, and whether we hunt turkeys or whitetails, much has changed in the way we hunt.

Not long ago, hunters who pursued elk in the bugle season were content to blow on a shrill call that essentially produced three or four notes. The call was a pipe or tube that did not accurately imitate a bull's whistle. Interestingly enough, the calls worked, proving the point that perfect bugle imitations aren't required.

What we DON'T know, however, is the effectiveness of the call. Would more bulls have been taken if the call had been more realistic? Did the call attract only the most vulnerable bulls who would have come in to practically any whistle?

Some veteran hunters swear by the old calls. My outfitter pal, Ken Smith, hunts the remote Selway Wilderness in Idaho. He's still using the call, and feels it does the job. Ken's success rate with the call has been excellent.

About a decade ago, it was discovered that diaphram

turkey calls would imitate a bull's bugle with much more realism than the old calls that you merely blow into.

The discovery added a new dimension to elk hunting. Word spread and manufacturers quickly produced diaphram elk calls, which are nothing more than turkey calls with the name elk call stamped on the packaging.

As the call was tested in elk woods, it became evident that it produced amazing results. More and more hunters reported that the calls were enormously successful.

But the call has a major drawback—it is difficult to learn how to use. Because it fits entirely in your mouth, your gag reflex makes you want to do just that — gag. Furthermore, if you aren't bothered by the object in your mouth, learning how to actually make the correct sounds often takes a great deal of practice. Some people give up and discard the call after weeks of trying.

Nonetheless, the call is the best on the market when it comes to imitating a bull's bugle. I'm often called on to be a judge during elk bugling contests — without exception the

As members of the deer family, an elk's antler's are extremely fast-growing. Bulls with antlers in velvet, as this one is, are encountered only by hunters in late summer. Velvet is generally gone by September.

candidates use diaphram calls.

If you haven't tried them and want to learn, buy an instructional tape cassette or video. There are plenty of each on the market that teach how to use diaphram calls.

The diaphram call can be used by itself or by blowing into a so-called grunt tube which is really nothing more than a short length of automobile radiator hose. The tube directs, magnifies, and deepens the sound. Practically every knowledgeable hunter uses a grunt tube.

Every elk bugles differently, vocalizing with a variety of notes. Some don't bugle at all, but grunt or whine. The grunt sounds like a puppy dog that wants attention. The diaphram allows you to grunt; most other calls do not.

Recently I took an elk that did not bugle. He grunted throughout our conversation, and I grunted as well. After a series of calls back and forth, he stepped into view and I managed to collect him at 40 yards distance with my .30/06.

There are other calls nowadays that are reasonably good

Bugling is a favorite hunting technique, and that's a major part of this book. Bugling in itself is effective only during the rut, which precludes all but bowhunters and those who hunt early seasons in backcountry areas and limited entry units.

These bowhunters look at a rubbed tree. The elk that worked over this sapling to a height of 8 feet probably wasn't that big. He no doubt bent the flexible sapling over while thrashing it. Nonetheless, a fine bull made his mark here.

imitations, but have different types of reeds. These are basically for hunters who cannot or do not want to use the diaphram. New models appear each year, and most work fairly well, although some aren't as durable as they ought to be.

Over the years, our observations of elk behavior has caused us to modify our strategies. In the past, the standard procedure was to bugle, wait several minutes, bugle again, wait, and move on if there was no response. Most of the time, bugling was done from ridgetops, where the call could be heard in the timbered slopes and canyon bottoms.

Many hunters are enlightened enough to know that the practice usually fails miserably.

Why? Primarily because elk often refuse to respond to a

Bowhunters pursue elk during the bugle season in every western state. This lovely bull came from Montana after having been called in with a bugle.

distant challenge. Unless the caller is in or close to a bull's territory, chances are good that the elk won't bugle at all, remaining content to just listen attentively.

I've had a number of experiences where elk were disinterested in my call until I moved within 100 yards of their location. Once, I tried bugling several mornings in a timbered draw that seemed perfect for elk. I got no answer, so I penetrated the thick blowdown near the bottom and tried bugling again. This time a bull bugled within 50 yards, and a few moments later I tied my tag to his antlers. It was obvious that he was living in the area because of the abundance of droppings and browsing, but he wouldn't answer my far-off challenge. It wasn't until I'd moved close to him that he was stimulated. When he finally bugled, he was hot and as fired up as any bull that I'd ever seen. Obviously he resented my intrusion into his domain and came out to teach me a lesson.

Another common error that we've recently discovered is being too timid once a bull responds. Many articles relate incidents where bulls charge the caller furiously, approaching within 20 yards or so. That might happen now and then, but more often the elk is somewhat neutral, unwilling to be the aggressor.

The standard reaction is for the hunter to call when the bull does. If the elk moves farther away, the hunter commonly believes he's done something wrong. In many cases, a LIVE elk cannot call another elk. Through trial and error, we've learned that being aggressive is far better than hanging back.

If a bull responds but it's a standoff and he seems to remain rooted to the spot, or if he moves away, take off in his direction. Don't worry about natural noise, such as breaking branches and rustling through leaves. Elk are noisy themselves, and expect another elk to make woods sounds. The noises to avoid are human voices, metallic sounds, or clothing scraping against brush.

Before you take off after the elk, watch the wind. He'll vanish for good if he smells you. As you run, bugle and break branches. Finally, make a stand and bugle again, this time scraping the bark of a tree with a handy stick. You'll simulate a bull thrashing a tree with his antlers, and sometimes this trick drives a bull wild.

By moving in on a bull, you might cause him to suddenly make an about face. Elk are often intimidated up to a point, and then they will refuse to retreat any more.

It's important to remember that there are three types of bulls you'll encounter: the herd bull, the solo bull, and the spike.

The herd bull is usually a tough character, because he's no doubt outbluffed or whipped other bulls for the rights to his harem. When he hears your call, he might be reluctant to face your challenge because he doesn't want to lose his cows. Typically he'll move off, taking his cows with him. By chasing him and bugling as you go, you might push him to his limit. A bull who has earned respect from his cows will often stop and meet his adversary rather than slink away and lose his prestige.

The solo bull can be the hottest or coldest bull in the woods, depending on his mood. He's by himself because he lost his cows to another bull or he wasn't aggressive enough to collect a harem. If you try for him when he's angry and defiant, he might charge straight in. But if he's timid and cautious, he could run out of the county.

Being aggressive with this bull often works, but another option is to run away, bugling as you go. The elk might think you're afraid of him and pursue you, confident in his supremecy.

The spike bull is easily intimidated, but he'll come to a bugle call out of curiosity more than anything else. Although the spike is a yearling, he's in high demand among hunters because he's superb table fare. Many people believe spike bulls are the best eating of all big game animals.

According to common belief, the bigger the bull, the deeper and hoarser his voice. That doesn't always hold true. The size and age of an elk has nothing to do with his voice, though a high shrill voice indeed identifies a younger bull most of the time.

Obviously, if you blow deep, brassy notes, you'll identify yourself as a mean old bull, intimidating everything around you.

Perhaps the old calls work well because they're much higher pitched than the newer calls, sounding like younger bulls.

Jim Zumbo took this fine bull during a November Montana hunt. Snow forces elk off their high country domain, requiring them to migrate to lower elevations. Some of the biggest bulls in the Rockies are taken during late hunts.

By far the imitation of cow sounds is the newest tactic in elk woods. Cows make a sound resembling the chirp of a bird or the mew of a cat, depending on your interpretaton. The advantages of sounding like a cow are immediately obvious.

Think about it. If a bull thinks you're a cow, instead of a challenging bull, a whole new scenario is possible.

Consider the herd bull. While he might run off from the bugle of a competitor, the cow sound might tempt him to come look at the new girl in the woods. The concept is not new in hunting.

Turkey hunters imitate a hen to call gobblers. When romance is rampant in the woods, the sound of a female could make all the difference in attracting a male of the species.

I believe a herd bull will look up a new cow because he's selfish. I've seen it happen while photographing elk during the rut. Dissatisfied with what they've got, a bull will often try to add more cows to his harem.

Lust will also attract a solo bull to a cow call. After being whipped or bluffed by other bulls, the cow's voice is a sweet melody. Because he falls in love quickly, the cow call often works like a charm, attracting the unsuspecting loner bull.

Spike bulls come to cow calls because they're still not quite weined from Mama, in terms of social attraction. They're often kicked out of their family group by a herd bull, and will try to join up with other elk whenever possible.

As in using bugle calls, the cow call should be done from a place away from roads and trails, especially in the midst of timber stands where elk live. The more you penetrate dense forests, the better.

Cow sounds are easily made by using standard diaphram calls. Instead of making the long fluted sound of a bull, you simply emit a soft chirp. There are also a number of calls made specifically for cows. The first was introduced by Don Laubach of Gardiner, Montana. Many hunters who were unaware of the advantages of making cow sounds tried the calls and reported amazing success.

Recently I came up with my own cow call, called Jim Zumbo's E-Z Elk Call. Made of very soft plastic, both calling edges are of different lengths, allowing calls of varying pitches to be made very easily.

The cow call works for obvious reasons during the breeding period, but one of its major advantages is the fact that it works after the rut as well. Because elk are gregarious, the sound of a cow will often bring in other cows and bulls. When the rut is over, bulls are no longer vocal. Bugling has no place in the woods, and might even spook elk.

Western states start their general firearms elk seasons after the rut is over to protect bulls that otherwise would be vulnerable. Most openers are in mid October and early November. Since bugle calls are ineffective, standard techniques such as stillhunting, stalking, driving, and others are required to find elk that are entrenched in timber. During this time, the cow call affords the only opportunity to attract elk.

Another option is to gang call. This is simply a technique where two or more hunters call at the same time, sounding like a small herd of elk. Cow calls can be easily varied in pitch by adjusting the amount of air you blow in, as well as the

Jim Zumbo watched this elk fall over and die. The bull suffered from starvation due to Yellowstone's 1988 fires and the prolonged drought which affected winter ranges. This is natures's way of dealing with wildlife. Agony and suffering is routine when nature does it her way.

amount of gap in the call. The gap is determined by biting down on the call. Cow calls are external, and are much easier to learn to blow than the diaphram device.

There are other important aspects of using the cow call. When walking through the woods, blow on it every few minutes. You'll sound like an elk to every other elk within listening distance, reassuring them when they hear you. The call puts them at ease, allowing you to get in close. Obviously elk will have your location pinpointed, but they'd do that anyway if you were merely walking along. It's virtually impossible to walk through elk woods without making noise, and noise is acceptable. Even when casually walking about, elk snap twigs and break branches. Another valuable option is the ability to stop elk if you've spooked them. When elk are suspicious of your presence, they'll commonly jump from their beds and run. By blowing on the cow call immediately, you'll likely confuse the elk. They'll stop in their tracks and look around, unsure of the danger. The tactic doesn't work well if they've smelled you, though I've been able to momentarily stop elk when I was positive they'd winded me.

If you can temporarily stop elk, even for a few seconds, you might have an opportunity for a shot. It could spell the difference between success and failure.

All sorts of new concepts will no doubt be uncovered in elk woods. By using these strategies, you might join the minority of hunters who score. Because only two of every ten hunters take their elk each year, a hunter must use every trick at his disposal to beat those odds.

Chapter 2

The Elk Woods

Understanding elk environments is just as important as knowing the quarry's behavior patterns.

Elk have a wide variety of habitats, from the Roosevelt elk which resides at almost zero feet elevation along west coast ocean beaches to the Rocky Mountain elk that lives at 11,000 feet or better in the Rockies.

Within those extremes, elk live in several forest types, each requiring different hunting strategies because of topography, abundance of water and food, hunting pressure, density of vegetation, and other factors.

Let's look at each major environment, and note some important factors that will help your hunt.

Sagebrush-Juniper: We generally think of elk as being animals of the high country — of dense forests overtopped by majestic snow-capped peaks. That's often true, but there are notable exceptions.

In several western states, particularly in parts of Arizona, New Mexico, Utah, Colorado, and Wyoming, elk inhabit very low elevations, usually around 4,000 to 6,000 feet. They live in vast expanses of sagebrush dotted with stands of juniper or a mix of juniper and pinyon pines.

Because of the arid climate, you'll normally find elk concentrated around water sources, and they'll seldom be far from cover. When they're undisturbed, however, they'll remain in the sagebrush for weeks where they're highly visible.

Hunting these elk might seem simple because they're readily seen prior to the opener, but don't forget that other hunters can see them, too. Once the season opens, hunting pressure will cause herds to vanish in the small juniper forests which are often quite dense.

Many herds are located in limited entry areas, so you'll need to draw a lottery tag for an opportunity to hunt. If you do, try to locate as many herds as possible, and check out waterholes, especially those in out-of-the way places. Find out about waterholes by perusing topo maps, and talking with cowboys, ranchers, sheepherders, game wardens, and employees of public land agencies such as the BLM and Forest Service.

Quaking Aspen Forests: These forest types normally grow at mid-elevational ranges, usually from 6,500 to 8,000 feet. The habitat here is often moist, with plenty of water in creeks, beaver ponds, and seeps.

The states with extensive quaking aspen patches include Arizona, New Mexico, Colorado, Utah, Idaho, and Wyoming. Plenty of public land offers hunting in the "quakies" as they'll locally known.

Aspen forests are a common habitat for elk, chiefly in the central and southern Rockies. Note the scars on these trees. They were "barked" by hungry elk who eat the outer layer.

Ponderosa pine forests offer a semi-arid environment in many Rocky Mountain regions. The forests are not as dense as others, and the trees are often scattered on grassy slopes and plateaus.

Elk will often feed in and around aspens which often support lush stands of grass. During the day, however, they'll usually move into bedding areas on northern points of ridges forested by Douglas fir stands.

If you hunt aspens before the leaves fall, elk might be hard to see, but after the foliage is gone there's often good visibility. An effective technique is to look for elk from a high vantage point such as the crest of a ridge, observing the aspens across a canyon or draw. Elk are often readily spotted as they feed and travel to and from bedding areas.

In some quaking aspen forests, water is somewhat scarce, but you can often locate it by noting the presence of livestock and following well-worn cattle trails. Much aspen country is grazed by livestock.

Ponderosa Pine Forests: This forest type is characterized by scattered trees with grassy openings throughout the forest. Ponderosas usually grow at about the same elevations as aspens.

This bull is partially visible in typical elk country -- spruce, fir, and pine trees that provide dense cover. Elk are at home in heavily timbered areas.

Because of the uniformity of feed, elk can be anywhere, but they're apt to be close to heavy cover, such as brushy draws and dense stands of young pines. Water is usually abundant, but in the lower reaches of pine forests it can be scarce, usually found in creeks and waterholes.

Depending on the density of cover, elk may or may not be visible from a distance. Much of the topography is flat in ponderosa country, preventing a good look from a vantage point, but in some places pines blanket sloping areas that you can see into.

Ponderosa forests grow in parts of all the western states, normally on south-facing slopes and in elevational ranges just beneath denser spruce-fir forests. In several areas, lodgepole pines are mixed in with ponderosas.

Cover as much ground as you can in open pine forests. Elk herds will be almost anywhere; it's tough to predict where you might find them. Get as far away from roads as you can, because elk will be in places overlooked by hunters. There's often good road access in ponderosa areas. The farther from roads you hunt, the better.

Jim Zumbo took this bull on a limited-entry Colorado hunt in 1988. Much of the country was in low elevations, where elk inhabitated sagebrush and juniper forests.

Dense Evergreen Forests: This is traditional elk country, composed of Douglas fir, alpine fir, lodgepole, and Engellmann spruce. These forests may grow in pure stands, especially Douglas fir and lodgepole pine. Alpine fir and Engellmann spruce almost always grows in a mixture. The latter two are often the densest, nastiest environments inhabited by elk, and the four species support more elk than the other types already mentioned.

In Roosevelt elk habitat in the West Coast states, other timber types make up the forest, including a variety of firs, cedars, and pines. Coastal forests are often the thickets of all, with extremely dense underbrush. Constant rain is almost always an important factor here.

Water is seldom a problem in evergreen forests, but forage is often absent. Elk must leave the forest daily to feed in clearcuts, grassy meadows or clearings, often called "parks".

Most of what you read in this book will relate to this type of forest, and you'll note that I often repeat myself many times about the need to get in the timber and forget watching or hunting the clearings.

This forest environment will make or break your hunt. Master the techniques, hunt hard, and you'll earn your elk. And in most cases you'll do exactly that . . . earn it. There are few easy hunts in the rugged, steeply-sloped evergreen forests of the West.

Chapter 3

Understanding Elk Behavior

It's no surprise that the most successful outdoorsmen are those who are most familiar with their quarry. The trapper who catches beaver consistently, for example, knows when and where the animals feed, how wary they are, and where they live. The fisherman must be just as astute. He must know how to read water, how to determine what the fish are feeding on, and how to outsmart the fish.

The elk hunter must understand his quarry just as the trapper or fisherman, but the hunter's chore is much more demanding. Whereas the trapper knows precisely where the beaver live in a marsh by locating the obvious house made of a mound of sticks and brush, and the fisherman can merely walk a stream bank or sit in a boat and have easy access to his quarry, the elk hunter must survey a vast chunk of western landscape and begin a long, tedious search. It might take days to see an elk, and some hunters never see an elk during an entire hunt.

This chapter will give you a detailed insight as to an elk's daily lifestyle pattern, starting in early fall, continuing through the rut, on into the transition or post-breeding period, and finally to the winter. Hunts are held during each of these four periods, and I'll explain the intricate relationships of elk that will give you a basic understanding of elk behavior. When you have a good comprehension of what makes an elk tick, you'll have a bit more of an advantage during your quest, just as the trapper and fisherman does.

The Prebreeding Season

Some states allow bowhunting in August and early September. During this period, elk are beginning to prepare for the breeding period, (also known as the rut or bugle season) which normally occurs the last three weeks of September and the first week of October.

During the spring and summer, a bull's antlers grow at an amazing rate. In mid to late August, the velvet coating begins drying up and shredding. It falls off, and the bull helps remove it by rubbing his antlers on brush and saplings.

In the summer, mature bulls are quite gregarious and hang out in bachelor groups, quite content to live together in a herd. As the breeding season approaches, however, bulls go off on their own, looking for cows. Initially, bulls just sort of check out the pickings, and aren't quite serious about breeding. They'll bugle a bit, but their hearts really aren't into it.

As part of the ritual, they'll visit a wallow, almost on a daily basis, and roll in the mud just as a pig would. The bull urinates on his belly, brisket, and neck while wallowing, and also urinates in and around the wallow. He thrashes nearby shrubs and trees with his antlers, rubbing so hard that the bark peels off, leaving a glistening yellow scar that can be easily spotted by hunters and other elk alike. Some biologists believe the wallow is a territory marker, used exclusively by individual bulls.

The Breeding Season

This is the marvelous period that appeals to those who love elk and elk country. Picture yourself being out there on a chilly morning, when quaking aspens are a riot of shining yellow, gold, and orange, and when frost glistens from lovely meadows, betraying the route of every animal that disturbs the jeweled glaze that coats every leaf and blade of grass.

Now imagine the spine-chilling sound of an elk's bugle call, echoing about in the sweet smelling breezes of the western mountains. This is the quintessence of autumn, a period of time that every serious big game hunter should experience at least once.

Elk are the most timber-oriented of all our big game species. The lodgepole pine forest shown here is typical habitat.

During this time, from early September to early October, mature bulls are dead serious about breeding. They locate herds of cows, driving out yearling bulls that often hang out with cows and calves, and defend their harems against other challengers.

Bugling is a constant activity during this period, and is performed for a variety of reasons. Bulls bugle to warn other bulls to stay away, they bugle to assert their dominance, and they bugle to reassure their cows.

There is a great deal of movement among cows during this time, especially when herds are active in late afternoon, through the night, and during early morning hours. Individual cows or small groups of cows and calves may wander away, regardless of the bull's antics or pleading calls.

Because much of the bull's activity is determined by the

Notice the shred of velvet hanging from this bull's antlers. He's ready for the rut, prepared to gather as many cows as possible.

cows, bugling is at its peak during those hours of cow movement.

This is the chief reason you'll hear more bugling early in the morning and throughout the night. Most observers recognize that fact, but I've never yet read this explanation. It makes sense.

Bugling is also much more active when a cow is in estrus (heat). Other bulls scent the receptive cow, and move close to the group. The herd bull remains busy chasing off other bulls, and, in fact, his romantic cow is often bred by a young bull who slips into the herd when the harem master is busy chasing away another intruder. I've witnessed cows being bred by an interloper a half dozen times.

Herd bulls will collect as many cows as he can. I've seen harems ranging from a single cow to as many as 86. The average is anywhere from eight to fifteen or so.

Remember that calves are mixed with cows, remaining with them throughout the breeding season. There is a great deal of vocalization going on between cows and calves, especially when the herd is feeding or moving about. There is little or no vocalizing when the animals are bedded during daylight hours.

Herd bulls often don't retain their dominance of the harem for very long. A more aggressive bull might come by and steal the cows by outbluffing or actually fighting, though the latter is rare.

When there's a confrontation between a herd bull and challenger, the scenario usually goes like this: the intruder bugles his intentions, moving closer toward the herd. The herd bull bugles back, rushing out to meet the opponent. The two bulls run toward each other, but stop when they're five to 25 yards or so apart. Each bull will thrash a nearby sapling, usually bugling in the process. By some intimidation factor that we humans haven't yet figured out, one of the bulls will turn and run. The victor is the one doing the chasing, but he

This bull is fast asleep. As a herd bull with a dozen cows, he doesn't get much rest during the bugle season. He's constantly active, except for short periods when he dozes during the day.

never really catches up, just going through the motions of being the tough guy.

The parallel march is another form of confrontation. Each bull runs alongside the other, maintaining a space of two or three yards apart. This might continue for several hundred yards, until one of the bulls breaks the pace and runs off, or when one of the bulls actually lowers his antlers and charges. The other bull will meet the charge or run off.

When antler contact occurs, the fight becomes a pushing and shoving match. The loser normally is the one who is being pushed backward the most, and eventually he retreats with the victor in hot pursuit. Occasionally a bull will suffer a serious or even a fatal wound from a tine puncture during the battle, but often only their pride is hurt.

In most cases, the more aggressive bull is the winner, whether the confrontation is a bluffing game or a real fight. He is a master of intimidation, coming across as being mean and ornery.

Notice I said a more AGGRESSIVE bull rather than a BIGGER bull. What does the word BIGGER mean in the world of elk? Do you suppose an elk judges an adversary by the number of points he wears, or the mass and length of his opponent's main beams and tines?

I think not. A bull has no idea what he wears on top of his head. He has no way to tell if his rack is more prominent than another's. It's the temperament of the challenging bull that means everything, provided we're matching bulls of about the same body size and age class. I've seen a modest five-point bull with fire in his eyes charge angrily into a herd, while the much larger six-point harem master ran off, totally intimidated by the smaller bull.

Generally, the oldest bulls have the most massive antlers, and they're often the most aggressive. But it isn't necessarily true that the largest bulls end up with herds of cows, or even the biggest herds of cows.

Post-Breeding Season

When cows are no longer in heat, the yearly romance is over. This usually occurs in early October, though there are exceptions.

A typical harem. The herd bull beds close to his cows during daylight hours.

Bulls will often stay with herds of cows or they'll live solo. Because most general hunting seasons begin after the rut, hunting pressure forces elk to stay in the timber longer than usual, coming out only in the evening to feed in grassy meadows and clearcuts.

During this period, vocalization among bulls ceases, but cows and calves continue their chatter. If you were to blow a bugle this time of year, you'd be wasting your time, but there are exceptions, depending on when you were hunting. If it's mid-October, you might arouse a bull who believes you're consorting with a cow in heat. He's not apt to approach, but at least you can locate him, if he bugles, and move in his direction, using the bugle call or cow call or both.

Since bulls no longer keep harems, groups of cows tend to bunch together in larger groups as fall progresses. Bulls also join up together, forming herds of two to ten or more.

Bulls lose a great deal of weight during the breeding season. Survival is a priority, since they must regain plenty of pounds before winter sets in. They feed extensively during the post-breeding period, but not to the point where they'll

After the breeding season, bulls are no longer interested in cows or bugling. Survival is of the utmost importance as they gain back the weight they lost during the rut. This bull eats on and off throughout the day, pawing through the snow to find adequate feed.

endanger themselves. Practically all their feeding occurs at night if they seek open meadows, or they'll remain in the timber if enough grass is available.

Late Season

During most years, mid-November is the start of winter. Heavy snows blanket the high country, requiring elk to paw through snow to reach food beneath it.

Elk begin migrating at this time, moving to lower elevations, often following well-established routes. Winter ranges are often located in valleys, riverbottom areas, ranches and farmlands, and other places that have light snow cover.

In some regions, elk remain on high, windswept ridges where the constant wind blows snow away, leaving grass exposed.

Late hunts are often the finest for someone who wants a big bull, especially where elk migrate out of refuges such as national parks and onto areas where hunting is allowed.

By this time, mature bulls are grouped in bull herds, and cows, calves and younger bulls gather in very large herds numbering 100 or more.

On the famous National Elk Refuge in Jackson, Wyoming, an average of 8,000 elk migrate in each fall and spend several months eating hay. As the snow recedes in the spring, they begin a reverse migration, slowly working their way back to summer ranges in higher elevations. This is the typical pattern of elk everywhere that migrations occur.

Notes

— Chapter 4 —

The Bull Elk

(NOTE: This chapter, as well as the chapter on cows and calves, details the behavior of elk from the time they're yearlings to the time they're mature. This is one of the most important chapters in the book, because it reveals why bulls act and react to other elk. As you read, try to grasp the intricacies of the bull, how his brain works, and how you, as a hunter, can use bugle calls and cow calls to your advantage. By knowing how and why bulls react to your calls, you can plan strategies based on their actions. Your interpretation of what you see and hear in the elk woods, and reacting accordingly, is a vital aspect of being a successful hunter).

Elusive. Big. Handsome. Charismatic. These are just a few terms used to describe a bull elk. And if that isn't enough, there are more. He lives in the finest mountain country in the hemisphere, and when he bugles his throaty scream, his voice symbolizes all that is primitive and wild. His antlers cause man's eyes to gaze in wonderment and awe, and when his flesh is prepared for consumption at the dinner table, he has no equal.

No wonder so many hunters revere and cherish the splendid bull. In the opinion of tens of thousands of hunters, he is as perfect as a big game animal can be. There are no close seconds.

The bull comes into the world at about 28 pounds in late May or early June. A spotted calf, looking not unlike a deer fawn, but much larger and darker in color, he is closely guarded by his mother, who shares her microenvironment with other elk.

As soon as he takes his first breath, the bull squeals, making a sound that we call a chirp or mew. All calf elk make the sound, as do the cows and bulls. For the most part, however, we associate the sound with the cows and calves.

If the bull calf is hungry, confused, or frightened, he'll let out a series of plaintive squeals. You can bet Momma will come running to protect or comfort her youngster.

The biggest threats to his young life are disease, malnutrition, and predation. The latter is chiefly caused by black bears, who sense when he's about to be born. The bear follows the cow, attacking and devouring the calf as soon as it's born.

Once the calf is on its feet, the cow hides him as she feeds, and returns to its location when he needs to be nourished. In this stage the calf exudes very little scent, which is nature's way of protecting him from predators.

By fall the young bull is weaned, remaining with his mother and the rest of the herd. He usually stays with the group until the following year, when he leaves on his own or is evicted by a big bull during the breeding season.

The Yearling or Spike Bull

During the second fall of his life, the bull is called a yearling, even though he's really a year and a half old. Most big game animals are classified in the half-year category because they're born in the spring. When hunting season rolls around, they're one-half year old, one and one-half, two and one-half, and so on.

Most yearling bulls carry spike antlers, which are a pair of single antlers generally running from 10 to 20 inches long. Because many young bulls do not attempt to rub the velvet coating off, it often remains for the life of the antler.

Some yearlings develop a small fork, or even three or four small points at the tips of their spikes. Biologists feel this is caused by genetics or nutritional factors.

The young bull is sexually mature, but he isn't quite sure about the art of romancing cows. What little ardor he has cannot compare with that of older bulls, and he's no physical match either. As a result, he is quickly separated from his

This bull is sleek and fat, and is well-prepared for the bugle season. Jim Zumbo photographed him when the bull walked over to investigate Zumbo's cow call.

mother and the herd that he lived with for 16 months when the big bull comes visiting during the rut. It is no contest when the older bull makes a run at him. The spike skedaddles, and often joins up with other yearlings, lives solo for a couple months, or just hangs around the edge of the herd.

At his age the spike can bugle, but his call is short, high-pitched, and sounds nothing like that of an older bull. In fact, the spike commonly makes the chirp more than the bugle sound.

In some areas where heavy hunter pressure consistently claims older bulls, spikes have been known to service cows. If a spike bull is among cows in heat, he will get the breeding job done.

After the breeding season, spikes evicted by herd bulls will rejoin the herds, living together and migrating to winter ranges in large groups.

The spike's antlers are shed in March or April. As soon as they drop, a new growth forms, and within days the young bull is sprouting a new rack, this time with branched antlers.

Bulls rub their antlers vigorously on saplings and brush. This is a normal part of their behavior. During the course of the breeding season, an individual bull will thrash several dozen trees.

The Raghorn

With his spikes gone forever, the raghorn, or two and one-half year old bull, enters a different world. Come fall he will be sexually mature, and he will, because of nature's urgings, take part in the breeding ritual, or at least make a valiant attempt.

By the time summer ends, the raghorn will typically wear antlers boasting four or five points. He is yet no match for bigger bulls, but he is king of the hill in regions of heavy hunting pressure, especially where spikes are protected. If that was the case, he was spared as a yearling, and survived the season. Because spikes are protected, hunters focus all their efforts on legal bulls, and few survive the season. In some areas, none survive, leaving the raghorn as the oldest bull in the herd, until he too is harvested.

This bull now has a voice that sounds like a standard bugle, though some observers say it is not as hoarse and deep as that of a bigger bull. That may or may not be the case. Every bull has his own voice. Some raghorns have brassy, deep voices, and some big bulls have thin, reedy voices.

During the early and mid-summer months, the raghorn often hangs out with other bulls of the same age class. He lives much of the time in higher elevations, often in and around breezy meadows where flies are not as abundant as in lower elevations, and he stays out of the thick timber to protect his delicate antlers that are rapidly growing.

When the velvet starts to peel, the bull begins to feel the breeding urges. Bugling occasionally, he selects individual saplings or bushes and rubs the velvet off his antlers. He works only on that sapling or bush, often destroying it in the process by breaking the stem completely or stripping away all the branches. Later he'll work over another.

Wallows are important at this time as well. Biologists believe bulls use wallows to cool their ardor, and possibly to mark territories. The bull literally rolls about in the wallow, coating his pelt with fresh mud and urinating on his body and in and around the wallow. He'll rub the bark off nearby trees, often bugling as he does so.

Zumbo encountered this bull during a September snowstorm. He was a solo animal, unable to win cows from rivals. Though he has a fine rack, he apparently wasn't aggressive enough to outbluff or outfight other bulls of equal size who had harems.

The raghorn runs himself silly during the breeding period, trying to establish his own harem. In areas where there is an abundance of bigger bulls, his efforts will probably be in vain. Larger bulls will have the cow population divided into harems.

If the raghorn is unsuccessful, he's often called a satellite bull, though this term can be used for older bulls who are also loners.

The lonely raghorn is frustrated and angry. He's been chased off by herd bulls, unable to gather his own cows, and spends much of his time in isolation or traveling a great deal, hoping to locate some straggler cows.

Frequently a raghorn will hole up in a spot, bugle his rage, and stay in that area for days. Other times he'll run 10 miles or more a day, bugling and carrying on.

He'll also harass a herd bull, often with one or more raghorn companions. He'll know just how far he can go, running toward the herd of cows, and being chased off by the master. Now and then, while the herd bull is off chasing another intruder, the raghorn will slip in, quickly locate a cow in heat, and breed her. When the big bull returns, the raghorn has accomplished his lusty activity and is gone.

If the raghorn hears another bugle during his wanderings, he may swiftly retreat because he doesn't want a confrontation. He's totally intimidated because of his previous experiences with bigger bulls. On the other hand, he might charge straight in to the bugle caller, ready to size up his adversary and outbluff him or even fight. Another reaction is to remain where he is, bugling and grunting, refusing to leave his little secluded spot.

A bull's mood changes rapidly. One moment he might be meek and reclusive, in another he might be ornery and aggressive.

If he hears a cow elk, he might throw caution to the winds and run in to investigate. Or, he might stealthily approach, checking to see if the cow is with a herd bull, or unattended.

In the event the raghorn wins a herd of cows, he'll behave just as a much older herd bull, protecting his cows from other bulls, and by bluffing and fighting challengers.

When the breeding season passes, the raghorn eventually

Spike bulls are either kicked out of the herd by the boss bull, or are allowed to remain at the outer edge of the harem. They will commonly answer cow and bull calls.

joins other bulls, including other raghorns and older bulls. As a group they'll migrate to lower elevations if necessary, and stay together for most of the winter and following summer. His antlers will be shed in the spring; at that time he may live alone or with small bull groups.

The Herd Bull

If the raghorn survives the hunting season and the winter, he develops more massive antlers, each beam bearing five or six points. When the breeding season arrives, he is a formidable adversary, fully grown and ready to challenge other bulls for cows.

The bull behaves essentially the same as he did the

previous season. Throughout the summer, he goes through the antler-rubbing and wallowing rituals as before. Then, when the rut arrives, he's at a sexual peak, ready to breed. This year, he'll be a match for other bulls and will likely win his first harem of cows. In early September he'll break away from the companion bulls he lived with all summer, seeking herds of cows. At this point he isn't concerned with locating cows in heat, because the heat period occurs later. All he wants is to collect cows and keep them, breeding them as they come into estrus later on. He bugles as he travels about.

Once he finds a band of unattended cows, he'll assert his dominance by bugling, displaying his antlers in threatening fashion, and basically taking over the herd. He'll stay with them continuosly, eating and sleeping little.

If he can't find unattended cows, he may challenge the herd bull, hoping to win the harem. He does this by bugling as loudly and brashly as he can, and approaching the herd. As the herd bull runs toward him, both bulls will usually thrash a sapling with their antlers, or march parallel with each other, until one runs off. If an actual fight develops, the bull that pushes the other around may win, or one of them might suddenly lose his courage and run off.

While all this is going on, much vocalization occurs. Bugling is almost nonstop, except during the fight itself. At that time, the bulls are rack to rack, grunting, shoving, and trying to gain the advantage.

In areas where there is a healthy number of mature bulls, three and a half-year and older bulls may find themselves as satellite bulls. They aren't aggressive or courageous enough to win a harem.

These can be the hottest bulls in the woods, rampaging about until they triumph and run off a herd bull, or remain solo until the breeding season is past.

They can also be the coldest bulls as well, lying tightly in a thicket, refusing to respond to other bugle calls. If those calls come closer and closer, however, the bull may resent the encroachment of an intruder, and become so irritated that he'll leave his hideaway and meet the challenger.

The herd bull is often a coward if he hears a challenging bugle from another bull. He'll likely answer back, and move

Fighting is not common, but bulls sometimes meet head-on to win a harem. Usually there are no injuries, but at times bulls can be severely injured or killed by a rival's sharp antler tine.

his cows away, sometimes at a walk, sometimes at a trot. He might travel completely out of a drainage before stopping.

Other times the herd bull will put up with no nonsense, leaving his cows and rushing off to meet the intruder. His reaction, either way, depends on how aggressive and confident he feels at the moment.

A herd bull will stay with his cows for one or more weeks after he breeds the last cow to come in heat. Then he'll strike out alone for a period of time, or join up with other bulls.

Because of the frenetic pace of guarding his cows, he's lost much weight. He spends the rest of the fall eating voraciously, gaining back as much weight as possible to withstand the rigors of the upcoming winter.

When snow falls heavily in his mountainous environment, he migrates to winter ranges with other elk. If the winter comes early, he is one of the first elk to die of winter stress because of his severe weight loss during the breeding season.

Notes

Chapter 5

The Cow Elk

Few hunters consider cow elk when they think of elk hunting. In reality, most elk states require large numbers of cows to be harvested to keep populations at the carrying capacity of the habitat. Furthermore, the activities of cows are interrelated with those of bulls. Knowing about cow behavior patterns is important to the complete elk hunter.

There are some interesting myths about the role of cows in the breeding scenario. A primary one is the cow's attraction to a particular bull, generally one who has superior antlers. As the story goes, the cow selects the bull she wants, forsaking all others.

My observations, along with those of others who have watched elk intently, strongly reject this possibility. Cows are bullied by a dominant, aggressive bull, pure and simple. She and her calf and other herdmates have no choice. When a bull wants his cows to move, he moves them by making threatening gestures with his antlers and quick forward steps. If the cow doesn't move, which is rare, he runs at her rapidly with his antlers tilted to the side, and she moves — quickly.

The notion of cows selecting a bull is simply not the case. As I'll explain later, however, some cows have a stubborn streak and will merely walk away from the harem master, no matter what he does. Such instances are rare, but I've seen it happen.

A few years ago, a photographer asked me where she could go to photograph elk in their natural environment. I made a few suggestions, and she called me a couple weeks later.

"Those bulls were mean and nasty," she complained. "I

Though cows are controlled by the herd bull's actions, some cows refuse to be dominated. Zumbo photographed this bull as the animal tried in vain to encourage an independent cow to rejoin the harem. She refused, and crossed the river where she disappeared in the timber.

couldn't believe how they ran cows ragged all over the place. It was almost cruel. Those cows should have been defiant."

The photographer was a feminist, which is certainly her right, but she was being a bit anthropomorphic by suggesting that the cows should have stood their ground, rejecting the bull's incessant attacks. That's not the way it goes in nature. Humans can alter their relationships as they choose — wild animals adhere to the instincts they've followed for thousands of years.

Another myth is that a herd always keeps a cow posted as a sentry, watching for danger while the group feeds. That's not so, either. Cows are always looking for danger, more so than bulls. Their maternal instincts compel them to watch out for enemies, because they've done so since they had their first calf. A bull has only to watch out for himself. He's done so since he was born, because he had to protect nothing but his own hide.

This is not to say that bulls are dumb compared to cows — they're simply not as sharply tuned to the environment.

This cow yawns with disinterest as the bull walks by to check her out.

That's why you'll often see one or two cows looking about when the rest of the herd is feeding. It's their nature. If you watch long enough, every cow in the bunch will glance around now and then.

According to another myth, cows come running when they hear a bull's bugle. I've yet to call in a cow with my bugle, and I've yet to hear of another hunter doing it. That's not to say it will never happen, but it's not part of normal elk behavior.

Cows are pretty complacent critters. During the heat of the bugle season, they seem completely disinterested in the antics of the bull. They mosey around, feeding calmly, and are controlled only by the herd bull's aggressiveness. Only when each cow comes in heat will she become interested in the bull. She will stand still and allow the bull to mount and breed her. The whole process takes less than five seconds. That's about all the interest she ever has in the bull. Five seconds a year . . .

Calf elk make the same chirps as cows. It's possible that cows respond to cow calls because they think a calf is vocalizing.

When in heat, the cow does not run from the bull, but stands and allows him to approach.

When a cow is close to being in heat, the bull is constantly near her, often getting her up from her bed by brandishing his antlers, and basically harassing her until she finally allows him to mate her.

In areas where herds are numerous, a cow will often simply take off and leave to join another herd. Often a bull cannot turn a truly stubborn cow, no matter how frantic his actions.

Once, I watched a cow leave a huge herd bull who had 81 cows and calves in his harem. She simply took off and walked across a river while he bugled and whined and basically made a fool of himself. He followed her halfway across the river, bugling and pleading, but she wouldn't return.

Sometimes a cow or a small group will bolt and run, leaving the herd bull frustrated as he tries to chase them down.

According to some new research, there's a bit of trading that goes on during the night. Cows leave herd bulls, and head for other herds or just wander about. I believe this is the

The actual mating act lasts several seconds. It is the only time the cow shows interest in the bull.

primary reason that bugling is much more frequent during the early morning hours. After an evening of activity, with cows moving off and splitting from herds, the harem master runs about feverishly, trying to regain control and regroup his ladies.

Cow elk are extremely gregarious. You'll seldom find one alone, unless she's been temporarily split from the herd by hunting pressure or is having her calf.

In May or June, each gravid cow takes off for a secluded area where she gives birth to a single calf. Twinning is extremely rare. Shortly after the calf is born, the cow rejoins the herd. She hides her calf as she feeds, returning to it when it's ready to nurse.

The calf makes a high-pitched chirp, which is nicely imitated by the standard cow call. When stressed or in danger, the calf makes several squalls. This type of vocalization continues into the fall months during hunting season.

Mimicking a distressed calf has obvious advantages, no matter when you try it in the fall. An inquisitive cow who hears your calls may come looking, and bring the whole curious herd with her, including the bull.

The cow also makes the chirp, and it can be of different pitches. I believe the basic difference between the cow and calf vocalization is the frequency and duration. The calf seems to call more often, with longer chirps, though it's easy to be confused. I don't think it's possible to precisely define each call, because they're so similar.

Merely using the cow call has so many logical implications that any hunter who doesn't use it is really missing out on an important tool.

It's necessary to blow the call softly if you're trying to imitate a cow. A loud call will more likely imitate a squalling calf. Don't blow the call repeatedly; wait 10 seconds between each soft mew, and vary the pitch as well. Blow the call three or four times, and then wait several minutes.

Cows and calves vocalize when they're active, seldom when they're bedded. You'll get more response in early morning and late afternoon hours.

Calves are generally weaned by hunting season. They're capable of surviving on their own if the cow is harvested during hunting season. Cows must be harvested from time to time to control elk populations.

Zumbo called this cow elk within 10 yards of his location by using a cow call.

This cow is at full alert. She barked when she sensed something amiss, and ran off, taking the whole herd with her.

By using the call when you're merely walking through the woods, you'll put any elk within earshot at ease. They'll think you're other elk, and will allow you to get closer than usual. They'll have you pinpointed, however, and at some point will figure out the betrayal, but at least you'll approach much more closely.

Notes

— Chapter 6 —

When Bulls and Cows Talk

There are far more myths surrounding a bull's bugle call than any other aspect of elk hunting. The call itself is a charismatic, romantic, thrilling sound that emanates from the deepest and most pristine of our western forests. It's logical that we let our imaginations get carried away as we try to explain this wonderful vocalization.

Elk hunters learned long ago that a bull elk will often respond to a man-made bugle. No doubt Indians imitated the sound to draw elk close to their primitive weapons, and early settlers also learned how to call. Today, we've refined the technique to the point where elk calling has developed into somewhat of an art.

Despite our progress, there are many unanswered questions about elk vocalizations. Relatively few scientific studies have been done. Most theories come from avid hunters and wildlife observers. If there's an "art" to elk calling, it's really based on a number of experiences that have led to some broad conclusions.

A bull's vocalizations change as he grows older. As a calf he chirps, just like a cow. As a yearling he makes a short, shrill bugle, and he also chirps. As a mature bull, his bugle attains the long crescendo, often ending with so-called grunts.

He can and does chirp as a mature animal, though many hunters don't realize it. Most chirping occurs when the bull is in the company of other elk, so it's difficult to tell which animal is making "cow" sounds.

During the rut, a bull also makes a strange sound that is

Bulls bugle for many reasons. This bedded herd bull is bugling as if he were yawning. Zumbo observed him bugling while bedded a dozen times over the course of a morning.

seldom heard, unless you're within a few yards of him as he herds his cows about. It's a hollow plopping sound, which sounds something like several wine bottles being uncorked. I have yet to hear of a hunter who has imitated the sound, and I know of only two or three people who have heard it. I haven't seen the sound described by other authors. I suspect that if the noise was imitated within earshot of a herd bull who refused to answer a bull or cow call, he might come unglued and charge straight to the sound.

Let's put one famous myth to rest right now . . . You've no doubt read that a big bull has a much deeper, hoarser, bugle than a younger bull. I learned, after observing hundreds of bulls, that the statement is about 75 percent correct. It's quite possible to be fooled.

For a number of years I photographed elk in Yellowstone National Park with my good pal, Gabby Barrus, of Cody, Wyoming. In fact, it was Gabby who initially introduced me to Cody, and when I realized the lovely town was central to the best big game hunting in the West, I moved there!

Gabby and I often tried to guess the size of a bull by listening to its bugle. In late afternoon, herd bulls tended their cows in meadows near highways, oblivious to traffic and people. Invariably, other bulls would bugle from within the timber, and eventually stride out into the open. Quite often, Gabby and I were dead wrong in our guesstimate. Sometimes a pipsqueak bugle turned out to be the voice of the King of the Mountain. Other times, a brassy, throaty, deep bugle was made by a modest bull who couldn't hold a candle to the big boys.

It's not a bad idea to have calls of varying pitches. Sometimes a bull will respond to one, but not another.

It's true, too, that shrill, high-pitched bugles account for plenty of responses from bulls. I have an old call made of thin tubing that makes a very high bugle, similar to the pitch of the old three-note calls. Those calls work well, even though they seem to be far inferior to the modern diaphram calls. Perhaps bulls are indeed less intimidated and feel less threatened by a high-pitched call.

During the day, bulls are restless. They bed among their cows, but get up often to take a walk through the herd, as if to assure his girls that all is well.

Another popular myth perpetrated by some folks who should know better is the notion that a bull's bugle hits four definite notes, then falls off to a series of grunts.

That's most definitely not the case. To see for yourself, simply listen in the elk woods. You'll quickly learn without a doubt that every bull bugles differently. You've probably heard that there are no two snowflakes exactly alike. Neither are there two bugles exactly alike.

Recently I was in Alberta's Banff National Park, photographing elk and sheep in September. It was prime time — elk were bugling their brains out.

About a dozen bulls inhabited the ski slope just above the Banff townsite. It was interesting to listen to them. Their notes were as varied as their antlers. Some bulls let out with a blood-curdling scream that had only two notes, some just grunted, some seemed to bugle forever, others bugled for two seconds or less.

The next time someone tells you a bull bugles a four-note melody, look the person in the eye and ask him what he's been reading — or drinking.

Some critters vocalize almost perfectly. Consider the honk of a wild Canada goose or the soft yelp of a hen turkey. There's almost no variance to their vocalization. Listen closely to the next bull elk you hear — you'll immediately note differences. I've concluded that bulls generally bugle under six different circumstances, though there could certainly be more.

As a herd bull, he bugles almost as if he were yawning, and does this when he's lying in his bed. He seems to be saying something like: "I'm okay, you're okay. Just leave me alone for the time being."

He also bugles to reassure the ladies in his harem that all is well. He seems to say: "I'm the boss, girls. Behave yourselves and everything will be fine." This vocalization is made as he feeds lightly with his harem, or merely stands around surveying the situation.

Another type of bugle is made by the herd bull as a response to a challenge by another bull. He's really rankled at this time, and may look directly at the challenger (if he's in sight), or toward the direction of the challenger's bugle, or he may look away and bugle. He seems to say: "Come on over,

These bulls are involved in a serious confrontation, but the ritual ends up as a bluffing contest. The bull on the left has a harem. The challenger finally ran off.

fella. Make my day."

A herd bull also bugles if some of his girls get out of line, wandering away from the herd. This vocalization is a firm warning, possibly saying: "Get back here, sweetie, or you're in big trouble."

Another bugle is made by the challenger whose vocalization is directed toward the herd bull. He knows the herd bull is in the vicinity. He could be saying: "I know you're there, big boy, and I want some of the action. I'm coming over to steal your girls."

Lastly, a bugle is made blindly by a solo bull. He vocalizes as he wanders through the forest, either looking for a challenger, or generally feeling sorry for himself. He's saying something like this: "Hey — everybody out there. Here I am, and I'm upset."

Please understand that these are my interpretations. I made them by closely observing lots of bulls, and I'm offering human rationales for elk behavior, which is not completely accurate. Yet, that's the best we can do. Since we can't

This raghorn, or 2 1/2 year old bull, is usually solo during the breeding season, though sexually mature. He just can't compete with older, larger bulls.

communicate with elk and ask them all the unanswered questions, we'll have to speculate.

The bugle call is described many ways. Typically, a writer will say it sounds like this: "Eeeeeeeeeeunhh."

Okay — if that's how the writer wants to describe it, that's his or her business. But the word, or any like it, doesn't really do much for the bugle. No words can describe it. My advice to you, if you want to learn what a bull sounds like, is to:

a) Visit live elk in a park, zoo, or refuge during the bugle season, or

b) Buy or rent a video tape on elk bugling, or

c) Buy an audio cassette tape on elk bugling, or best yet,

d) Hunt elk during the bugle season.

The word "grunt" is used to describe the sounds made by a bull immediately after the last note of the bugle. In reality, these sounds are more like whines — something you'd expect a pampered puppy dog to make when he wants something. To me, the word "grunt" resembles the guttural sound made by a pig, or even a bull moose. Nonetheless, the term has been used so long in reference to elk vocalization, that we all use it.

The complete elk vocalization includes the bugle followed by one to six or more grunts. This is the standard format, but plenty of bulls bugle without grunting, and some grunt without bugling. An individual bull will vary his sounds, depending on his mood and social status.

The frequency of an elk's bugle depends on a number of circumstances. If you believe my opinion stated above that bulls bugle for at least six reasons, you should understand that any of those scenarios will contribute to his mood, and, of course, the amount of vocalization will be directly attributed to that particular mood.

Now then, here's the big question that we all ponder... when is the peak of the bugle period, and what starts it, stops, it, slows it down, and hastens it?

You've probably heard that a good hard frost will really get the ol' boys tuned up, that a full moon is bad, that warm weather and rain slows 'em down, and on and on.

This herd bull displays the typical aggressive posture when he's tending his cows. He's on the fight, and quickly intimidates his harem.

So what's the truth?

The professionals who study elk reproduction have not quite decided on the factor or factors that trigger bugling activity, though there are two major possibilities. One is photoperiod, which means the amount of light in a day. Once the photoperiod attains a certain level, the rut begins. Another theory is related to calf drop the previous spring. In other words, when cows give birth to calves, their estrus or heat period will begin so many days afterward. The latter theory appears to be the most widely accepted these days.

Does local weather affect the rut? I believe it does, but only in that vocalization is increased or decreased. Breeding activity remains the same regardless of the weather.

Most veteran elk hunters agree that cold nights and frosty mornings seem to enhance vocalization. As a general rule, I go along with the observation. I also concur that periods of extended rainfall, as well as abnormal heat, will decrease vocalization.

But it's impossible to predict what elk will do based on weather, or ANY factor. While it's true that most of the hunts I've been on during hot weather were frustrating because of lack of elk activity, some of my most memorable hunts occurred during very hot days. Granted, they were rare, but nonetheless, they occurred.

Likewise with rainy periods. I've had all sorts of experiences in Idaho's Selway, where it's tough to see the sun because of rain clouds. Yet, on a hunt during a particularly bad rainy period, I heard more bulls bugle than on any other hunt I've ever been on.

The old adage of being out where the elk live rather than in a tent or cabin certainly applies. Anything can happen in the elk woods, and usually does.

Some hunters believe the moon affects elk behavior. The theory goes that elk will feed more during moonlit nights, and head for their bedding areas in the timber earlier than usual. As a result, hunting will be poorer during periods of the full moon.

I have a hard time believing that. Practically all big game animals have superb night vision. They don't need the moon to see. Too many times I've ridden horses on nights so utterly

A very alert, busy bull. Note the wet pelt. He's worked himself into a sweat while tending his cows and running off challenging bulls.

black I couldn't see my hand one inch from my eyes. Yet the horse always followed the trail precisely, gingerly stepping over logs, detouring around brush, crossing creeks, and otherwise impressing the heck out of me. If a horse can see during pitch black nights, so can elk.

Cow vocalization is not nearly so dramatic as that of the bull. Essentially, their chirps are meant for internal communication within the herd.

Cows chirp to their calves frequently, and vice-versa. These sounds are probably reassurances, or even scoldings. When calves are upset, they often squeal loudly and frequently. Cows probably chirp to locate their calves. Most animals can identify each other by their vocalization, even though it all seems to be the same to us.

Most cow vocalization occurs when the herd is up and about, feeding or walking. As such, you'll hear the sounds early in the morning and late in the afternoon when elk are active rather than bedded during the day.

Cows bark when they're alert to danger. This vocalization can be described just as it is — it's truly a bark. You'll never mistake it when you hear it. The bark is a signal, just as a beaver slaps its tail on the surface of the pond. Every elk within earshot of the bark will be instantly alert, and will usually begin running. Sometimes elk will bark and stop and look for several minutes, confused by the danger. They're unsure of what's happening, and will walk stiffly about. They seldom calm down at this point, but eventually run off.

Mature bull elk chirp, especially when sparring. I wasn't aware of this behavior until I was camped in a national park and saw it for myself. In the middle of the night I heard cow chirping just outside my camper. I looked, and under the light of the restroom I saw two four-point bulls pushing and shoving each other about. They were chirping and squealing as they sparred, and I was intrigued.

Would you believe that cow elk bugle? I saw that for myself, too, and I wouldn't have believed it if I hadn't seen it. The cow that bugled had a calf, and she was with a herd of eight other cows and calves in an open meadow. There was no question that it was she that bugled. I watched her open her mouth and let go with a perfect melody, but it was not followed by grunts. I have no idea why she bugled, though I've often tried to figure it out.

To me, elk vocalization is exciting to hear, and to watch, if possible. Understanding it, or at least making good guesses based on knowledge, is a most valuable assist in our hunting efforts. You don't have to be a perfect bugler to call an elk. It's much more important to try to interpret what the elk are saying, and then responding intelligently, either with the bull call or cow call. And that, readers, is the essence of this book. If you make logical strategy decisions, you'll have a far better chance of scoring.

Chapter 7

The Trophy Bull

As the old saying goes, a trophy is in the eyes of the beholder. Each hunter has his own definition of a trophy. Perhaps a small four-point elk taken with a bow and arrow means more to a hunter than a bigger bull taken with a rifle. I once took a five-point bull with a bow and arrow during a tough Montana hunt. I have a great deal of respect for that animal, and he'll rank high on my trophy list.

This chapter will explain how to care for your trophy, from caping the head to preparing it for your taxidermist. It will also offer tips on actually determining a trophy-status bull when it's on the hoof. As you read this book, tips on trophy hunting will appear in practically every chapter. This one basically tells you what to look for and how to take care of your animal.

If possible, photograph your elk in the event you're successful, not only for a memento of the hunt, but as a guide for your taxidermist. He'll be able to make a more realistic mount if he can see a photo.

Unfortunately, most photos don't capture the trophy in good taste. Take some time to properly arrange the picture before you snap the shutter.

The very best pictures are taken as soon as the animal expires. He'll have a fresh look, and will show up well.

Carry a small camera in your pack. Be sure it's protected from the weather, unless it's waterproof. A Zip-Loc bag will seal it nicely.

Photograph the bull before it's field-dressed. Otherwise the body cavity might show, and you'll probably have some unwanted blood in the photos. Don't waste time taking the initial photos, because you don't want to delay field-dressing any longer than necessary.

If the animal is in the shade, drag it out in the sun if you can. That can be a mighty big chore and perhaps impossible if you're on a steep slope and you're alone. A trophy bull will require at least two or three or more grown men to drag him on the LEVEL, never mind uphill. Otherwise, use a flash if it's in the shade. Pose yourself with the animal from a variety of positions.

Try to keep the sun in your face; if you're wearing a hat, tilt it so the sun hits your eyes, or your face will be dark in the photo. Be sure the photographer's shadow isn't in the picture. This is a special problem early in the morning and late in the afternoon when the sun is low and shadows are long.

If you don't have your camera with you at the site of the kill, try to position the bull in front of a good background when you get it to camp or to your home. Be sure the body cavity doesn't show. Place the elk in an acceptable position, or just photograph it from the shoulders up.

Never take an animal's photo if it's in the bed of a truck or the background is cluttered. Try to place the elk where the background will accentuate its features. Above all, show respect and sensitivity when you photograph a dead animal. You'll be much more proud of your photos, and others will enjoy looking at them if you take some precautions with your camera.

Two major scoring systems are used for North American big game: Boone and Crockett and Safari Club International, known as B&C and SCI respectively.

Basically, the B&C system awards trophies on mass and symmetry. Penalties for unsymmetrical antlers are subtracted from the total score. The SCI system is concerned with mass rather than symmetry. No penalties are deducted.

Study the record book for each system to learn scoring requirements. Look over the charts carefully, and then look at actual mounts. You can see them in taxidermy studios, sporting goods stores, hunting clubs, and other places. If possible, actually score the antlers to give you an idea of the system. This is an important requirement if you want to be a trophy hunter — you MUST be an expert at scoring. Doing the measuring yourself is sort of like driving a car as opposed to being a passenger. As a passenger, you aren't paying much

Ed Rozman poses with the biggest bull in the world, killed by John Plute in Colorado before the turn of the century. Note the size of the bull. He dwarfs the owner, Ed Rozman, who is of average height.

attention, and might not be able to retrace your route in a strange area. As the driver, however, you are alert at all times, and quickly learn how to get around in an unfamiliar area. You learn by doing — no matter what.

Four factors determine a bull's antler configuration: age, genetics, feed, and the animal's general health. Of those, age is the critical component. An elk could have nutritious foods, and excellent bloodline, and be of good health, but if he doesn't live long enough, he can't grow trophy-sized antlers.

A bull requires five or more years to grow truly large, massive antlers. The more years he survives, the larger his antlers.

If you're interested in a trophy animal, check the record books to identify areas producing the most trophies, but be sure to consider the most recent entries. Many areas that produced trophy-class bulls in the past no longer give up record animals. Colorado is a good example. The world record bull was taken near Crested Butte, Colorado near the turn of the century, but Colorado is no longer a prime trophy elk state. Too much hunting pressure allows consistent harvesting. There

Steve Ferguson with a fine Alberta bull that scored in the 360's. Steve and Jim Zumbo hunted the area east of Banff National Park, where Clarence Brown took the third biggest elk in the world. The hunt was a fundraiser for the Rocky Mountain Elk Foundation.

are some good bulls in limited entry and wilderness areas, but truly huge bulls that might qualify for the record book are rare.

A trophy earns his antlers by escaping hunters for several seasons, or by living in a protected area and then making himself vulnerable by leaving that area, such as animals that live in national parks and migrate out during winter.

If you're truly a trophy hunter, you must not only be hunting in a prime area, but you must have the restraint to hold your shot when a good animal presents a target, but he isn't quite trophy material. It takes a great deal of will power to allow a fine animal to walk away, and you should have no regrets afterward if you allow it to happen. Very frequently a hunter will pass up a fine bull and never see another one as good. Don't look for sympathy if it happens. Make your decision and stick by it.

Polls show that most nonhunters approve of hunting for meat, but disapprove of merely hunting for a "head for the wall" or a rug.

With some exceptions, as in the case of bears and cougars, (though both are edible except for bears feeding on carrion), trophy animals are harvested for their meat. In fact, states have "wanton waste" laws which require the edible portions of animals to be transported from the kill site and consumed.

From a biological standpoint, trophy hunting does not, except in rare instances, affect the genetic quality of a herd. By the time a bull is big enough to be a trophy, he's already sired several females over the years. His bloodlines are well distributed throughout the herd. The exception is very heavily

Jim Zumbo with a fine trophy. The bull scored 353, and was taken during the peak of the bugle season.

hunted areas of sparse cover where males are consistently harvested each year.

It's practically impossible to harvest all the mature bulls from an area having substantial escape cover and restrictive seasons — those animals grew that big because they're smart. Enough of them survive to maintain the desirable genepool. Notice that I said substantial escape cover and restrictive seasons. If cover is lacking, elk can indeed be easily harvested. If seasons are long, extending into late November, a disproportionate number of trophy elk are often taken as they leave the upper elevations. However, severe winters occur infrequently. Big bulls often survive several years, until they're eventually forced out of upper elevations by deep snow.

A trophy on your wall means more than just a "stuffed head". It represents the memories of a grand experience, not only the kill, but the magnificence of the country you hunted, the camp, your companions, and every aspect of your adventure. Be proud of your bull, and don't be dismayed by the comments of others who cannot understand your attitude.

You can preserve your trophy three ways: by mounting the antlers on a plaque, by having it done in a neck or shoulder mount, or by having a life-sized mount done. You can do the first technique yourself, but the last two require special skills.

Remove the antlers by sawing them off with a standard carpenter's saw or hack saw. A chainsaw works well if you have one. Do this chore when the animal is fresh, instead of allowing the head to sit for weeks; otherwise the brains will have a most distastful odor as you cut open the skull.

Before sawing, peel the hide away from the place to be cut with a sharp knife; or it will interfere with the saw.

Make your first saw cut about an inch behind the antlers, cutting down toward the top of the eye sockets. Make the second cut across the bridge of the nose at the bottom of the eye sockets. When the two cuts meet, the antlers and skull plate should come free.

Cut away all hide and tissue, and boil the skull plate to loosen any residual flesh. Don't allow the antlers to touch the boiling water, or they'll become discolored. Discard the dirty water and boil the skull plate again in clean water. Next, submerge the skull plate in very cold water, which prevents it

It's important to take proper care of your trophy. Jim Zumbo carefully saws the antlers from the skull.

from turning yellow later.

When the skull plate is dried, bolt or screw it to a plaque. You can buy kits which have plaques, screws, and leather or velvet coverings. Some hunters leave the skull plate exposed, as in the European mounts; others cover the plate and allow only the antlers to protrude.

If you want to have a neck or shoulder mount made, your animal must be properly caped. This process requires care, or the cape will be ruined.

Take proper precautions as you field-dress the animal in the field. When making the incision to remove the entrails, stop at the brisket if you want a shoulder mount. Never cut the bull's throat to bleed it or cut away the windpipe.

Before caping, photograph the head from different positions. This will help the taxidermist later when he mounts your animal.

To cape, start by cutting completely around the body ahead of the ribcage. At the top of the back, make a straight cut toward the back of the head. Stop between the antlers and make a cut to each antler, using a screwdriver to push the hide

Caping an elk head requires care and knowledge. Here, Montana outfitter Jack Wemple skins a head for one of his clients.

away from the antler burrs, cutting as you go. Next, cut from the brisket down to the foreleg at each knee. Keep cutting, pulling the hide toward the head inside out as you would a sock. Carefully free the hide from the face, being careful to include the eyelashes, ears, and nose. If you don't feel competent doing this, skin just the neck and shoulders, cutting the head off under the chin. Your taxidermist will do the rest.

Salt the hide immediately, or quickfreeze it if you can't deliver it to a taxidermist right away. Don't fail to salt it if it isn't frozen. Hair will slip after just a day or two. Don't spare the salt. Use at least a pound or two.

If you think your bull is big enough to make the record book, don't saw the antlers off unless you know what you're doing. If an antler is loosened from the skull plate because your saw cut was errant, the head will be invalid. It cannot be officially scored.

Additionally, guard the antlers with your life, and take them to a trusted taxidermist. A record class rack is worth a great deal of money these days.

Before you go on your hunt, determine what it takes for a bull to be a trophy. Look over the scoresheet intently and note what parts of the antlers score heavily. Also note where the penalties come from.

Long main beams and tines count heavily, as well as massive beams. A wide spread is important, since it adds to the score. The fourth point back is called the royal. If it appears to be at least 18 to 20 inches long, you're looking at a dandy bull. Some big elk have only five points. They'll never go in the record book, unless they're exceptional. You'll need at least a six-point to qualify. The more points, the better.

Remember that all elk look big. You must really know what you're looking for to take a trophy. Less than a dozen bulls make the record book each year.

Many hunters who read my *Hunt Elk* book or magazine articles ask when I prefer to be elk hunting. My answer is always the same — during the bugling season. But if you asked me the time to hunt trophy bulls, I'd unhesitatingly take the latest season around, when snow forces elk out of their high country domain. And you can bet I'll be using my cow call when I hunt during the late months.

As I mentioned earlier in this chapter, I'm not going to get into strategies for trophy bulls here. You'll see them elsewhere in the book. Furthermore, the state by state listing will give you an insight on where to go.

Notes

— Chapter 8 —

Bugling — Are We Overdoing It?

How often have you heard someone say that too many people are using calls these days, and we're educating bulls to the point where they won't respond? This chapter addresses that possibility, and offers some options.

A bull elk can be one of the most frustrating of all our big game animals. Other species can produce exciting hunting moments, but elk quickly and easily make human life miserable. Nothing else quite compares with them.

You'd think that a critter that weighed one-quarter to one-half a ton would be reasonably simple to hunt. Unfortunately, they are not. In fact, as I've said elsewhere in this book, hunting success for elk is by far the lowest of all our western big game species. If we average all the elk states, about 20 out of 100 hunters take an elk each year.

But what about the bugle season, that wonderful time when bulls are hotly pursuing cows and challenging each other for rights to the ladies of the species. Shouldn't elk be a whole lot easier to hunt?

There's no question that hunting during the bugle season affords a unique opportunity. Because of the option of attracting elk with a call, the hunter has the advantage of pursuing the animals when they're vulnerable. Timber-loving elk can be urged out into the open where they can be seen.

That's not to infer, however, that using a call will insure success. In fact, plenty of hunters conclude hunts each year during the prime bugle period without so much as seeing or even hearing an elk.

It's easy to blame the elk's unpredictability for his no-show performance. There are times when the most skilled hunters are utterly baffled by elk and their whimsical nature. Quite often the big animals behave in a manner that defies logic.

Lately there's a theory being voiced among hunters that suggests we're educating elk to recognize that bugling means danger. The opinion holds that bulls have been conditioned by too many hunters using calls, and the animals simply refuse to respond.

To analyze that possibility, we must first consider the changes in elk calling today. Are there really more hunters using calls these days, and are those hunters truly alerting elk to the point where calling has lost much of its effectiveness?

Until the 1970's, most elk calls were tubelike whistles that yielded a high-pitched, shrill call that hit three or four notes. Many hunters made their own calls out of a piece of garden hose, a willow branch, or a chunk of plastic pipe. I experimented with all three, and found their melodies to be equal to the store-bought varieties.

In reality, however, the calls were a poor imitation of the real thing. Grunting, which is a series of whines made by most bulls at the end of the bugle melody, was almost unheard of by most hunters, who were content to blow on the whistle and settle for whatever happened.

Then came the diaphram call, which was really a turkey call that nicely imitated elk as well. Word spread quickly, and several manufacturers raced to produce the calls for western hunters. When used with a grunt tube, the call came as close to mimicking elk as humanly possible. A big drawback was the difficulty in learning how to use the diaphram call, but many hunters picked it up quickly. Today, thousands of calls are in use.

Manufacturers quickly realized that not everyone could use the diaphram call, and invented other types of calls that had an external reed. As a result, there's no excuse these days for not being able to closely duplicate a bull elk's bugle.

That being the case, it's obvious that we've perfected elk calling to a point where it's a highly effective technique. More elk hunters are indeed using calls more skillfully and realistically.

This bull is tuned up and ready to go! However, he is quickly wised up to continuous calling, so it's important to try other options as suggested in this chapter.

Are we truly wising up elk because of the proliferation of calls? I think we are in some instances, particularly where hunting pressure is heavy, but I'm convinced that the lack of response from bulls to calls is largely a result of factors other than too many hunters using calls.

"Bulls aren't bugling like they used to," a friend told me recently. "I think they're getting smart, and we're creating a different animal because we bugle too much."

My pal is a good hunter, but I don't agree entirely with his theory. The last four falls have been unseasonably mild. In fact, it's been downright hot during the elk rut.

Most observers believe that elk vocalization is affected by weather. Warm temperatures and extended rainy periods seem to suppress bugling, though there are notable exceptions.

One of the most active bugling days I've ever experienced occurred during a dismal, rainy week in Idaho. Despite the incessant rain, bulls were bugling everywhere. As I said, however, that was a rare day.

Heat is often blamed for adversely affecting bugling, and I've heard people say that hot weather interrupts the rut. I disagree strongly, and so do wildlife biologists. The reproductive urge of any species continues according to various factors, but weather isn't one of them. Animals breed when it's time to do so.

However, vocalization in itself is very definitely affected during hot weather, but that doesn't mean that the actual breeding behavior is stopped. Bulls still maintain harems, and carry on as usual.

I believe that hot weather prompts elk to bugle more at night, when air temperatures are cooler and hunting activity is absent. Regardless of the weather, elk are always active during the nighttime hours, as are all big game animals.

Hunting pressure can't be blamed as a major factor that suppresses bugling in most areas, primarily because few hunts are open during the rut. Exceptions include bow seasons, limited entry, and wilderness hunts. In those cases, there are comparatively few hunters afield, though some popular areas attract unusually high numbers of hunters.

Without exception, western states open their general rifle seasons after the rut. When woods are crowded with hunters,

Jim Zumbo with a bull he took while shooting his video, HUNTING BUGLING ELK. This bull required some finesse, but he readily came to the bugle challenge.

the bugle period is over. Calls are useless, and are a waste of time. About all you'd accomplish with your bugle is to attract another hunter.

In places where bowhunting is popular, excessive hunting pressure indeed can turn off bulls, just as too much predator calling wises up coyotes. It doesn't take much to educate a bull. He quickly becomes savvy to calls, particularly if he's winded or seen a hunter.

I don't think elk refuse to respond to calls that are not terribly authentic for the mere sake of accuracy in the melody. I've heard too many elk make bad calls. At times, I've sworn that the bugle I heard was made by another hunter, and was amazed to learn it was a bull.

But what DOES turn elk off, I think, is the continuous presence of hunters. It doesn't take long for bulls to equate calling with humans, especially if the calling follows the same pattern. Too many hunters bugle from familiar areas. Hunters who call from ridgetops, well-used pack trails, roads, and other easily accessible areas are making a big mistake. Elk know

Don Gobel, president of Browning, (standing), looks through binoculars while hunting in Canada. He hunted a wise old bull for four days, and though he closed in on one occasion, the bull managed to escape.

those locations, and are wary of them. It's no mystery that bulls won't respond to callers in those circumstances.

A typical scenario goes like this: A hunter bugles from a ridge early in the morning and gets an answer from a bull. The elk bugles several times, and then fades into the timber until he quits entirely.

The hunter tries again the next morning, and the bull repeats the performance. At some point the bull might become alert to the hunter or other hunters in the area, refusing to respond at all. He's wary, and probably won't be tempted, no matter how good the caller.

Careless hunters contribute to a bull's education by allowing the wind to carry human scent to the elk, or by being seen or heard. If that hunter tries a bugle call, be assured that the bull will avoid him and probably leave the area.

If bulls are wise to bugling, what are your options? Obviously it's not always possible to leave the area and find a "fresh" location.

The most sensible thing to do is to be aggressive. Leave the traditional bugling spots and penetrate the heavy timber and rugged terrain where elk live. It's a common mistake to ignore an area if no bulls respond to your bugle. Quite possibly an elk will be home, but you'll have to get into his backyard to get him interested.

Bulls will often remain silent when they hear a bugle, even if it's made by a LIVE elk. In that case, you need to invade his territory. Once you do, don't be surprised if he comes looking for you with a vengeance.

In many forested areas, it can be 10 to 20 degrees cooler along a creek bottom than the upper mountain slopes. Bulls like to inhabit those drainages, especially if there is no road or pack trail along the bottom.

Hunters are often reluctant to walk to those canyon bottoms for three reasons. They don't want to climb back out, they don't have the gear or inclination to pack an elk out if they get one, and they don't want to deal with the very thick vegetation that often grows in the canyons.

Yet those are choice spots for elk. To outsmart a bull, you must outsmart other hunters, too. That usually means hunting in places that other people avoid.

I recall a hunt a few years ago that had all the makings of a failure. Bulls weren't bugling, despite the fact that I was hunting during prime time. After bugling into a canyon for several mornings and moving on when I heard no response, I decided to hunt the canyon itself.

By noon I called in a big six point bull who hadn't bothered to answer me during my prior efforts. I shot him only when I got so close he couldn't stand it. Until that happened, I would have sworn there was no bull in the canyon.

Other hunters also bugled from the ridge into the canyon, and I'm sure the bull was wise to us.

Another option is to listen for elk at night. Take a walk, shining your flashlight only when necessary. Stick to trails or roads if you're worried about getting lost. Elk lose their fear at night, and will often bugle within hearing distance of roads.

By listening to them in the dark, you can get a general fix on their location and try them in the morning.

Cow calling is another option. Imitating a cow is just catching on in the hunting fraternity. Bulls might be used to hearing bugle calls, but they might quickly investigate the new girl on the block.

The cow call often works on both herd bulls and loners. Herd bulls are among the hardest to call because of their reluctance to leave their harem. Upon hearing a cow call, however, a bull will often leave his herd to investigate.

Loner bulls are also vulnerable to cow calls for obvious reasons. A bull who has no cows during the breeding season is unhappy. He'll often run straight in to the cow call, whereas he might be completely intimidated by the bugle call.

One of the biggest mistakes hunters make is being too timid. When you blow the bugle call, blow it frequently. If a bull answers and moves away, don't be fooled into thinking you've done something wrong. Most hunters will back off and try the bull later.

Don't do it. Run straight for the bull, provided there's plenty of cover and the wind is right. He won't be expecting that behavior from a hunter, but he will from another bull. Bugle as you run, whacking branches and rustling brush as you go. The more you sound like a challenger, the better. Remember, if elk are wary because of too much bugling, you

Jim Zumbo with a bull that refused to respond to a call until Jim unknowingly invaded the elk's living quarters. After several days of unsuccessful calling from a ridgetop, Zumbo walked within 100 yards of the bull's lair and easily called the bull, who was mighty upset to hear an intruder in his territory!

must dare to be different.

Like all big game, elk are conditioned to human behavior. Though we don't give animals the credit for being able to reason, they certainly are capable of learning by experience. I don't think there's any question that elk are extraordinarily wary in areas where calling is frequent. But I don't think those animals are necessarily impossible to hunt either.

A bit of flexibility and effort on your part will give you the edge. Go after the elk where they live, and use varied techniques. Anything you can do that other hunters don't will break the regular patterns. You could very well beat the dismal odds and collect your elk, even in places where hunter traffic is heavy.

— Chapter 9 —

Actual Hunt Strategies

This chapter is intended to present hunting scenarios, including all possible factors that may affect an elk's response. After considering all the information for each scenario, I've offered a number of options.

It's important to understand that every confrontation in the elk woods is different. What works in one situation might not work in another. Elk are unpredictable, especially during the bugling season, so it's important to try various methods if the first one fails.

Throughout this book I've tried to explain that hunting successfully with calls doesn't mean you must be a champion caller, or that your call must duplicate a bugle as closely as possible. It's much more important to be able to size up the situation by listening to the vocalization, and then responding with a workable strategy. Then, if that strategy doesn't work, try another. Some of the options listed here don't include much calling. You must apply techniques according to the situation at hand.

Using the cow call doesn't necessarily mean that you'll be making decisions based on listening to elk. As you'll see, many situations will allow you to use the call effectively in the quiet woods.

There's a very important strategy that is so consistently effective that I'm going to address it again, even though I've done so elsewhere in ths book. That is — at every opportunity, when nothing else seems to work, BE AGGRESSIVE. The biggest error made by hunters is being too timid. Many people, including some good outfitters and guides I've known, bugle too infrequently. Additionally, plenty of hunters will listen to a bull retreat, assuming the hunter has made a mistake, or his calling is poor. As a result, he shakes his head, figures the bull is too wary, and heads out of the woods.

DON'T EVER BELIEVE IT! ASSUME THAT EVERY BULL IS CALLABLE, NO MATTER WHAT HE DOES. I don't know how many times I've seen bulls walk away from LIVE bulls.

So how do you be aggressive? First, DO call frequently. If the wind is blowing or you're hunting near a noisy creek or in heavy timber, call every five minutes or so. Another aggressive technique, as I've explained before, and I'll do it again, because it's SO VERY important, is to quit calling from trails, roads, and ridgetops. Get down there where the elk are! Cross the stream, hike up the other mountain, wander around canyon bottoms. Try every place that an elk might be hiding, and that will be precisely where other hunters don't go.

Aggressiveness also means literally running at the bull, even at a fast trot, if required. Depending on the circumstances, you can bugle as you run, use the cow call, or scrape a branch against the bark of a tree, simulating another bull. Don't be afraid to make plenty of noise as you run, but avoid human or metallic noises. Break branches, shake sapling trees, make as many natural sounds as you can. Of course, consider the wind direction as you approach.

When you call, always be prepared for an immediate reaction from an elk. Don't call from an area where you can't get a shot if you're a bowhunter. Don't lean your rifle against a tree. Have it ready — you'll never know when the quarry will show up.

When choosing a calling location, find a spot where you have fair visibility, but don't overdo it. Don't set up at the edge of a big meadow. Few bulls will cross a large opening, especially where there is other hunter activity. You might get away with it in wilderness areas or limited entry units.

By all means, be out there in the woods long before daylight. You might hear the bulk of the vocalization for the day prior to shooting light. You might not be able to see the animals, but at least you can mark their locations, and try them later.

Chuck McKay stalks elk in a dense forest. He walks carefully, using the cow call frequently to reassure elk within hearing distance.

Most vocalization will occur early in the morning and late in the afternoon. Make every effort to be in prime elk country during that time. Most hunters aren't very excited about walking out of the woods in the dark, but you should strongly consider it if you're really serious about your hunting. Obviously, make sure that you can find your way out in the night, by hunting near a trail, waterway, or other path.

Here are a number of different situations that you might encounter. My options are merely logical strategies based on past experience, common sense, and, above all, hopeful guesstimates.

Yes, you'll do lots of guessing. There's no exact science when it comes to hunting. DO dare to be different. Some of the wildest things have happened to me when I tried something strange. You'll never know unless you try it. Above all, don't use traditional techniques exclusively if they don't work. Elk are unique animals. You should be unique as well.

Though I could have listed dozens of possible situations, I didn't because too many would be confusing. Instead, I've come up with a few, all of which I've tried. Basically I've attempted here to merely illustrate the need to be different, to try various techniques and to use the cow call as well as the bugle call.

Situation #1

Date: August 25

Weather: Very hot and dry. Temperature reaches a high of 80, a low of 50 in the evening.

Vegetation: Quaking aspen, with Douglas fir on northern slopes at ends of ridges. Thick stands of oak brush on some south exposures. Plenty of grass in aspen stands and brushy slopes.

This bull is spooked, and is running from the photographer. Zumbo blew the cow call quickly, and stopped the bull in his tracks. If Zumbo had been carrying a rifle instead of a camera, the bull would have been his!

Topography: Mountainous, with moderate canyons and fairly gentle slopes.

Hunting Pressure: Few hunters.

Road Access: Roads are plentiful. Most major canyons and ridges are roaded.

General Description: It's bow season, and elk are not vocalizing. You've seen elk early in the morning and late in the afternoon feeding in the distance, but they don't respond to bull or cow calls. They seem to be whimsical, not adhering to any definite patterns. You suspect they're "timbered-up" because of the hot weather.

OPTION #1

If you've been listening during the early morning, late afternoon, and even during the night and hear no bugling, it's reasonable to assume that elk aren't vocalizing. They should be preparing for the breeding season however, and that and the hot weather should attract them to wallows.

Look for wallows around beaver marshes if any are present, or along sidehills, especially where there is a patch of lush vegetation. If cattle trails are in the area, follow them, because they often lead to waterholes.

If you find a fresh wallow with rubbed trees in the vicinity, try watching it from a ground blind or tree stand. If nothing happens over the course of a couple days, try bugling and/or cow calling. It's possible that a bull might be visiting the wallow at night, and is bedded close by. Your calling could bring him in.

OPTION #2

Since it's bow season, you don't have much of an option other than watching wallows or calling to attract an animal within bow range. However, you might try watching trails that you suspect elk are using. If you spot distant animals early in the morning, note which way they head for the timber when they're done feeding. Use a spotting scope or binoculars. By determining their route, you can set up within bow range, and ambush the animals as they come out to feed in late afternoon. They'll often use the same trail as they travel to and from bedding areas.

These hunters are listening for elk vocalizations early in the morning. If they hear no activity, they'll head for deep, cool canyons and use a bugle or cow call.

Situation #2

Date: September 25

Weather: Hot and dry. Temperatures approach 80 each day, drop to 45 and 50 in the evenings.

Vegetation: Typical fir, spruce, pine stands. Meadows are scattered in the forest, basically composd of evergreens.

Topography: Steep mountains, typical for the Rockies. Elevation is about 8500 feet.

Hunting Pressure: Very light. A few hunters are in the same area, but competition from them is light or nonexistent.

Road Access: Little to none.

General Description: You're hunting an early rifle season during the prime bugle period. As such, you're in a limited entry unit or a backcountry area, both of which offer early seasons to rifle hunters.

One morning, you bugle and receive a response within 300 yards. The bull seems interested, answering your call, but it appears to be a standoff. He stays where he is, and his calls become more infrequent. From the sound of his bugle, you have him pinpointed in a thicket on a steep sidehill above you.

A very slight breeze is blowing downhill, but you know that night and early morning thermals normally blow downslope. As the temperature heats up, however, the wind is apt to change, carrying your scent to the bull. You'll have to move fast.

OPTION #1

Quit calling for ten minutes, and walk up the slope at a diagonal, so your route will bring you just below the bull. Softly use the cow call, varying the pitch so you sound like more than one animal. Blow the cow call every two minutes or so, and don't be afraid to break a few small branches as you walk. The idea here is to make the bull think you're a herd of elk, with or without a bull. Remember, he heard you bugling, and now he hears only cows. He'll likely respond to your cow sounds by bugling at you. When he does, bugle back. Don't be surprised if he comes unglued and looks for you. If he doesn't answer, silently and quickly climb up the slope, making a wide berth of the bull's location. Watch the wind. When you feel you're 200 or 300 yards above the bull, try a bugle call. He might respond to you in your new location. If he does, but shows no inclination to approach, try the aggressive method. Rapidly move downslope, heading directly toward the bull. Stop every 30 or 40 yards, bugle and scrape a branch against a tree. Now you're simulating an agitated bull who's trying to pick a fight. Keep moving in, stopping every now and then, repeating the performance. Be alert, because this is one situation in which the bull might respond silently.

OPTION #2

Make a sudden attack on the bull from the beginning. As soon as you realize he isn't coming, charge straight up to his location, bugling and thrashing brush every 50 yards or so. If he remains silent, quit bugling, and try grunting, whining like a spoiled child. This often does the trick. He might not be able to stand your antics.

Situation # 3

Conditions are exactly the same as SITUATION #2. Same date as well.

General Description: Despite it being prime bugle time, the forests are absolutely silent. You can't believe it. Though you're out early in the morning and late in the afternoon, you don't hear a single bugle. It seems like there are no elk in the mountains you're hunting, though you see fresh tracks and plenty of rubbed trees. You know the elk are out there, but you can't locate them. It's a maddening situation, one that happens often in good elk country.

OPTION #1

Put your hiking boots on and head for the hills. It's time to find elk. First, consider the thickest blowdown country you can find. Walk through it, softly using the cow call every five minutes. It's impossible to be quiet, so you might as well sound like an elk. If you find a cluster of freshly rubbed trees, or three or four trees in a small area, use the bugle call. If there are any deep canyons without roads or trails in the bottoms, work down to the bottoms. You'll likely see plenty of sign, and

This bull is thrashing a tree. You can do the same when you're working a difficult bull. Grab a tree and shake it, or scrape a branch across the bark of a tree, simulating a real bull's behavior.

you might find some wallows. Bugle frequently as you move through the bottom — every five minutes is okay, if there's a creek present and the timber is thick, as it usually is. It's amazing how the topography, vegetation, and stream noises will absorb or screen a bugle call. In places, your call might not carry more than 100 yards. You don't necessarily have to look into only remote spots. What you need to find is country undisturbed by hunters. Sometimes the most obvious places harbor bulls because hunters overlook them.

OPTION #2
    Though the woods are silent, you can bet that elk are in the breeding mode. If they aren't vocalizing early and late in the day, they're probably bugling at night. Take a stroll from camp during the evening hours, listening intently. If you hear nothing, give a call with your bugle. Sometimes bulls will answer, even in the distance. If you get a response, don't bugle again. Since it's night, you obviously don't want to call in a bull,

just locate them. Night calling is a new approach, and hasn't really been well-tested. I've tried it a number of times, and it works consistently enough that I'm convinced that it's an excellent strategy.

Situation #4

Date: September 25

Weather: Cool, sunny days, highs in the 60's, frosty in the mornings.

Vegetation: Lodgepole pine, Douglas fir throughout. Some meadows.

Topography: Steep, with a number of canyons running throughout.

Hunting Pressure: Very light.

Road Access: Few roads. Most access is via foot or horseback

General Description: This is an elk hunter's dream. Bulls are bugling everywhere in the mornings, but the hunt is turning into a nightmare. Regardless of what you do, you can't call in an elk.

You try working two or three bulls each morning, and without failure they finally quit responding and fade away. You figure you're doing something very wrong, and wish you were a better caller.

Your calling probably isn't the reason you're getting no action. It's likely that you're hunting an area with a low bull to cow ratio. Each bull has a harem, and the herd bulls are quite content to stay with their harems and avoid a fight.

OPTION #1

Try the cow call if you haven't already. Avoid bugling, instead listen for a bull to bugle on his own. Approach his location as slowly as possible, and softly blow on the cow call. Keep it up, blowing every 10 minutes. Blow only once each time, but call lightly. Cows never bugle with any velocity. Be watchful for a silent bull. Often he'll come in without a peep. Possibly you'll have attracted a solo bull who hasn't rounded up a harem, and he'll sneak in quietly to try to claim the cow. He doesn't know if the cow is alone or with a herd bull, so he's apt to ease in to investigate.

OPTION #2

Try the aggressive route again. Charge after a bull who taunts you by merely bugling and staying put. Don't be afraid to really push him. Work the cover and wind effectively, and get as close as you dare. RUN — breaking branches, bugling, and thrashing trees as you go. Approach within 50 yards of the bull if you can, and go no farther. You'll never be able to precisely pinpoint his location, and he'll likely move around as well.

Situation #5

Date: October 20

Weather: Cool in the day, with highs in the 40's, dropping below freezing in the evening.

Vegetation: Aspens throughout in the mid elevations up to 7500 feet, spruce and fir in higher elevations.

Topography: Rolling country, with some extensive heavily timbered plateaus.

Hunting Pressure: Moderate to Heavy

Road Access: Extensive

General Description: Here's the classic opening day situation. The general hunt begins, with hunters everywhere. The rut is over; bugling is nonexistent. With so much competition from other hunters, you must try something unique, or be extremely lucky.

OPTION #1

If you'll take the first legal elk that comes along, consider using other hunters to drive elk to you. Early on opening morning, well before shooting light, position yourself on a high vantage point, preferably in a saddle or high on a slope where you have good visibility below. Stay there as long as you can — all day if possible. Hunters moving about are apt to spook elk and push them around.

OPTION #2

Get out your map or rely on your knowledge of the country. As I've said many times in this book, hunt areas least disturbed by other hunters. Few people will climb steep slopes.

There are various cow calls on the market. Zumbo recently came out with his own, as well as an instructional tape. (See Appendix for details).

Often you'll find elk in such places, and in the worst tangles of timber imaginable. The farther away from roads you get, the better. Use the cow call when you walk through the timber. Pay attention to every noise you hear. A pop of a twig could mean the silent approach of another elk. Be aware of every sound in the woods. Use the call most extensively when elk are moving from feeding to bedding areas and vice-versa early in the morning and late in the afternoon.

Situation #6

Date: November 10

Weather: Cold, with highs in mid-20's, dropping to around zero at night. Snow is present, from four to six inches in mid elevations to two or three feet in higher elevations.

Vegetation: Pine and spruce, with large open sagebrush expanses.

Topography: Steep to gentle slopes, flat areas on benches and lower elevations.

Hunting Pressure: Moderate

Road Access: Most roads closed by Forest Service. Access is via major road systems.

General Description: Because of heavy snow in the high country, you're convinced the migration has started. Few hunters are about, most of them glassing from vehicles for moving elk.

OPTION #1

Most elk will be traveling through the timber, and may move a short distance each day. Elk that normally live in lower elevations might not have started to move, because of the comparatively lighter snow cover. Prepare to walk several miles a day, cutting for tracks. If you're in good elk country, you should come across fresh tracks sooner or later. When you do, try to identify a bull's track (if you're after a bull) by the much larger track. Follow as long as you can, being as quiet as possible. If the woods are noisy, blow a cow call every now and then. Have essential survival gear in your daypack, and prepare to hunt right up to dark. Elk will normally begin feeding before dark because they'll be hungry in the cold weather and have to work harder and longer to find food under the snow. The key to this option is to walk, walk, and walk some more, and get out there as early as possible and to stay out as late as you can.

Notes

Chapter 10

From the Shot to the Dinner Table

The bull elk answers your call, and you spot him at the edge of the clearing. He's standing broadside 250 yards away, and you waste no time resting your pet rifle over a sturdy limb. He demolishes a tree with his antlers, and you feel he won't come any closer. It's now or never. The crosshairs have a bothersome waver because you're winded, but you draw a deep breath, hold as steadily as you can, and squeeze the trigger.

The elk lurches at the report, takes two quick steps, and disappears in the dense forest. You're sure of a hit, but as you work your way down to the spot you're nagged by the thought that the sight picture wasn't exactly where you wanted it when the bullet sped away.

Maybe you hit the elk too far back. You shudder and walk more quickly to the spot where he stood.

When you arrive, your worst fears are confirmed. A few drops of blood shine from leaves on the forest floor, and your careful trailing turns up more scattered drops of crimson. After you've gone 200 yards, you know your elk is wounded.

Now it's time to go to work. You're determined to find the elk, no matter how long it takes. If you go about it properly, you might very well catch up to the quarry. But then again, you might not. Trailing a wounded animal depends on your skill, perseverence, and, of course, the animal's condition and his ability to travel.

Once you fire at an animal, it's mandatory by all laws of ethics and humaneness that you immediately determine if it was hit, no matter how convinced you are that you missed.

Unfortunately, elk are left unrecovered in the field each year because hunters thought they missed, but many of those animals were perfectly hit. Because the animal doesn't fall immediately at the shot, some hunters continue on their way, completely ignorant of the fact that their bullet hit a vital organ and the animal is lying dead just a few yards away.

A heart-shot animal will often make a violent leap, kicking its back legs like a bucking horse before dashing away at top speed. Typically, the animal will expire within 50 yards. Blood might be absent, giving no sign of a well-placed bullet. An animal hit in the lungs will often stumble, falter, or fall to the ground, quickly recovering and running off. You can expect to find your prize within 200 yards, which is about average for lung-struck game. When hit in the paunch, the animal often hunches up, makes a wobbly step or two, and bounds away. You'll have your work cut out for you to find this one. If hit in the leg, an animal will often drop to the ground swiftly, and just as swiftly regain its footing.

If you're bowhunting, you can often see the arrow strike the elk, but then again, you might not, depending on the angle of the shot, position of the quarry, and your ability to see well enough through the foliage.

Any time an elk reacts to your shot, no matter how slightly, assume it is hit. Make the same assumption even if the animal DOESN'T react. Check out every shot, and if there's no immediate sign of blood, keep looking until you're convinced you indeed missed.

If the elk runs off after the shot, stand silently and listen to it as it travels. Try to determine where it's going, listening until the woods grow silent. If you made a vital hit, you could hear the animal crash to the ground.

Before you head off to find your animal, stop at the site where you hit him and try to figure out what might have happened. Try to retrieve the sight picture in your mind when you squeezed the trigger, and make an objective evaluation of where you might have hit him. (Elsewhere in this book I've included a chapter about a Canadian elk hunt where I almost left a dead bull behind because I couldn't find blood or the animal. It was a sobering lesson... by recalling the sight

So your elk is down -- what next? In this case, Zumbo worked two hours just to move the elk for field-dressing. This was one of his biggest bulls, weighing close to 900 pounds.

picture, I convinced myself I'd hit the bull and I found him a few minutes later.)

For a reference point, leave a square of toilet tissue on a branch at the spot where the animal stood when you fired.

There are varying opinions as to whether you should follow quickly or sit down and wait for a half hour or so, giving the animal a chance to "stiffen up and die."

From a physiological standpoint, the more you push an animal, the more energy it will use up and the more it will bleed. Remember too, that the quarry has been hit by half a ton or more of foot pounds due to your bullet's energy, and the shock from that hit will wear off as time passes.

A wound that bleeds profusely will usually stop or at least slow down if the elk isn't pushed hard or beds down. An arrow will continue cutting action while the animal moves, but will slow down as well when the animal stops. If the initial hit with an arrow is in a vital spot, however, many archers wait a half hour more or so before following, allowing the elk to bed and succomb to the major hemorrhaging that occurs.

If all this sounds confusing, just what do you do? First, try to determine where the animal was hit by looking over signs at the scene. Of course, even a doctor would be hard pressed to make an accurate evaluation, but some signs are fairly reliable. Bright blood usually signifies a muscular wound or one to an artery or vein. Bubbles or froth in the blood generally indicates a lung shot. If you see digested food or what looks to be paunch material mixed with blood, the elk has probably been struck in the digestive system.

Unless you think the animal has been hit in the paunch, most veteran hunters believe you should take to the trail immediately. A gutshot animal usually doesn't lose much blood, and is capable of traveling a long distance. By allowing it to settle down, you might be able to slip within range and finish it in its bed or when it flushes. The elk will be extremely wary, constantly watching its backtrail.

In every other case, get on the trail quickly to allow the animal to continue to bleed and lose energy. The onset of night is another reason to follow quickly, and you should obviously move fast if it's raining or snowing. If you're in woods crowded with other hunters, it behooves you to find your elk before someone else does. There is no written law that decides who lays claim to the carcass, whether the other party administers the killing shot or finds your animal dead.

The primary reason hunters lose a blood trail is lack of attention and inexperience at locating blood. A distinct trail is easily followed, but if the elk isn't bleeding well, you'll have a tough job to follow.

Let's assume no snow is present to help you keep track of blood. Once you've marked the initial spot where the animal was hit, take a cursory look at the possible routes the elk might have taken and check for obvious signs of blood. If there is none, start from the beginning, moving from one crimson spot to another. Scan the ground surface, but don't overlook blades of grass and brush. Sometimes you can be so intent at looking at the ground that you won't see blood on vegetation off the ground. Check the trunks of trees; animals will often rub against them as they go, leaving a smear of blood.

Once you've determined the general route, mark the trail with a hat, bandana, glove, or another tissue of paper.

Be prepared for a workout when you cut up your elk. It's no easy task to move a huge carcass from the woods to a road, trail, or camp.

Continue this process as you go, but don't carry on in hound dog fashion with your eyes rooted to the ground. As you move, travel as quietly as you can, constantly looking ahead for the animal. It could be dead, bedded, or leaning heavily against a tree.

If you flush the wounded elk from its bed, make a snaphot if you have a clear target. You have nothing to lose; the quarry is already badly wounded, and a finishing shot will be required to put him down for good.

If the blood trail seems to vanish completely, roll your sleeves up and prepare to work. Clearly mark the last place you saw blood, leave the general route you believe the elk took, and make a series of circles. At this point, work with the wind, since you have the option of planning your movements. A wounded animal can still smell. You'll push it farther ahead if it winds you.

As you circle, look for a prostrate or bedded elk, and check intently for clues. Besides looking for blood, check for fresh tracks. An overturned rock or log might indicate the flight path of your quarry.

If the circling technique fails, return to the last place you saw blood and start an intensive search for another clue. It's possible the animal quit bleeding momentarily, but started again a short distance away. Dog the trail with every ounce of concentration you can muster. Look at the area from different angles; keep trying to find the next telltale drop of blood.

In much of the West, the vegetation will open up somewhat, offering some visibility. Scan the area ahead of you with binoculars. You might see the elk bedded or lying dead.

Keep track of your location as you follow the trail. You'll be intent on looking for clues, and could get turned around. It might be difficult to find your way out of the forest, but most western terrain is easy to figure out. Landmarks are often visible, and drainages are easy to identify in most areas.

In the event that you've lost the trail for good or nightfall approaches, round up some help. Go back to camp and return with your companions as soon as possible.

If it's legal where you hunt, bring a hound back to track the animal. Be advised, however, that tracking hounds are forbidden in most western states.

Keep an eye out for predatory birds. In the West, magpies and ravens are quick to locate a carcass. Some hunters swear the alert birds are attracted by a shot, and come quickly for a look.

If nothing else works, you'll no doubt suffer guilt feelings and feel badly for wounding an animal. At least, however, you've tried everything you could. It's possible too, that the elk recovered, depending on where it was hit, or another hunter might have located and claimed it.

Wounding an animal is always possible, no matter how much you've hunted, but you can prevent it from happening in the first place by knowing how to shoot accurately and turning down shots that are questionable.

In some cases you can hit an elk perfectly, but it won't bleed at all. Follow the general direction that you heard the quarry travel in, keeping your eyes peeled for the animal on the ground. Plenty of hunters have walked within a few feet of their elk, never seeing it until they repeated the search or smelled it. Elk have a distinct odor that can be detected from a short distance away.

If you have enough help and the terrain cooperates, you MIGHT be able to drag a big elk.

Elk are extremely tenacious and are capable of absorbing a great deal of shock from a bullet. It's common for a big bull to be hit perfectly, yet stand there and look at you, or even bugle after being hit.

In that case, most hunters would shoot again as insurance, even though they're confident the first shot was in the vitals. Always shoot a second time if the animal doesn't go down. It might be superficially hit, or gutshot, regaining its senses after being struck. More than one hunter has fired at the quarry, hit it solidly and knocked it down, and watched it get up and run off.

As soon as you hit the elk, chamber another round, put the rifle at the ready position, and keep the animal in sight at all times. If it tries to get up, or manages to get partially up, quickly shoot it in the neck if you can.

When you approach the elk, keep your gun ready until you're certain it's dead. If not, do not attempt a Tarzan style coup de grace with a knife. An animal could spring to life and cause you profound problems. Take a careful aim and shoot it high in the neck, centering the shot so the vertebrae will be hit.

The old axiom, "the fun of the hunt is over when you pull the trigger" has never been more true than in the West. Whether you tag a 600 pound bull elk, a 300 pound spike, or 450 pound cow, you're apt to have a tough chore getting the meat out of the woods. You'll likely be faced with more rugged terrain than you're used to if you're a nonresident, and roads are few and far between as compared to eastern and southern hunting areas.

No matter WHAT the circumstances, field-dress the elk immediately after the kill. Bacteria works rapidly, and your animal will spoil unless you quickly cool the carcass.

The difficulty of your chore will be directly proportional to the size of the animal that lies on the ground before you, and the terrain. A big bull elk who falls belly down on a 40 degree slope will be a part of your worst collection of nightmares for years to come. An elk that hits the dirt 10 minutes before dark will also be not-so-fondly remembered, though those memories tend to mellow once the job is done and we relate the ordeal to pals in our living rooms.

Whatever size elk you take, your immediate objective is to unzipper the animal from brisket to anus and remove the entrails. The job is almost impossible unless the animal is lying on its back with its hooves pointed to the sky.

Positioning a spike bull or young cow isn't terribly difficult, but a mature bull might require some help. If you're alone, all you can do is push and pull, using sheer muscle to accomplish the job. If you're working on a steep slope and the road or trail is at the bottom of the mountain, you might want to roll the carcass down by using gravity before you field-dress it.

A heavy animal could hang up behind a rock or log as you maneuver it, but the closer to the bottom you get it, the less work to carry meat. By rolling it down before it's gutted, you'll prevent the cavity from accumulating dirt and debris, which is always a problem with a heavy animal.

If you've remembered to bring 50 feet of strong, lightweight rope, tie the elk to a tree before attempting to position it for gutting, especially if the road is above you. Every

In some areas, if you have no horses to pack meat, your only recourse might be to bone your elk into pieces and carry it out on your back, as Zumbo is doing in this photo.

extra yard the carcass slides down will be remembered afterward, and it will probably slide unless it's leaning against an obstruction on the forest floor.

If you're working on a big elk, you don't need a Bowie knife to do the job. Most veteran hunters use a simple pocketknife. All you're doing is cutting skin and muscle. The smaller the blade, the more precise your cut.

In the case of a bull elk, remove the sex organs first, UNLESS it's illegal to do so. Many western states require proof of sex, requiring you to leave the head or sex organs attached, and they want those items attached until the meat is at the locker plant or at its final destination. Almost no one keeps the head attached — be smart and leave the sex organs intact if proof is required.

Make the initial cut carefully, slicing through the skin somewhere near the sex organs. Cut just deeply enough that you sever the membrane between the hide and the intestines. When the slit is big enough, insert the first fingers of your left hand (if you're right-handed) into the cut, and push down on the intestines. With your knife blade pointed upward, follow the "V" made by your fingers up to the bottom of the rib cage, called the sternum.

If you want to cape the animal, end the cut a few inches below the sternum. Complete the cut from where you started, working to the anus.

As you work, you'll notice that the intestines will begin bulging out through the incision. Reach in and cut away muscles and tissues that attach the intestines to the cavity. Carefully pull as you cut, until you've freed the entrails, rolling or dragging them well away from the carcass as you work.

The heart, liver and lungs are protected by the heavy wall of muscle called the diaphram. Cut the latter until you expose the vital organs, then reach as far as you can with your left hand until you feel the windpipe at the bottom of the throat. As you grasp it, ease the knife in and cut the windpipe above your fingers.

When it's cut free, pull hard on the windpipe, slicing away tissue as you go, and the organs will spill out. If you want the heart and liver, cut them free and set them in a clean place, such as on a rock or a mossy spot.

The last step is to ream the anus. Carefully cut around the canal from the outside beneath the tail, reaching deeply with your knife. Avoid piercing the bladder which is just above the pelvic bone. If you do, urine will dribble on the meat, spoiling it wherever contact is made.

When the anus is completely reamed, pull it back toward the tail if the bladder is empty or nearly so, since the bladder and lower intestine will come with it. If the bladder is full, carefully grasp the tube between the bladder and anus and pull from the inside.

If you can't immediately transport the carcass and the weather is warm, drag it to a shady spot if you can. Place some wrist-sized branches on the ground and roll the animal on top, allowing air to circulate underneath. This is a critical step if the animal is to be left overnight, no matter how cold. The weight of the carcass pressing on the very thick hide will trap heat, even if the animal is lying on snow.

Wedge a stick into the chest cavity to spread it wide, and flop the hindquarters so they're exposed to the air. Cover the

If you're extremely lucky, you might be able to haul your elk out in one piece. This, however, is an exception!

carcass with evergreen boughs to keep birds away. Coyotes will seldom touch a carcass while strong human scent lingers, and it will usually take bears a while to find it.

If you have time, you might want to quarter your elk and hang the meat from a branch. This is almost always a job for two people, but if you're stout enough you might get the job done.

Because of grizzly bears, there are special regulations governing the way meat is left overnight in certain areas around Yellowstone Park's borders. It must be hung so many feet from the ground if it's a certain distance from a road or trail. Those rules may change frequently; check them before you hunt in that region.

Before heading out of the woods, be sure you can find the animal again. If in doubt, mark the location, as well as a trail out. A small length of plastic ribbon attached to branches is the standard technique; be sure to remove the plastic when you return.

If you're hunting in country with high bear populations,

look over the carcass from a distance when you return the next day. A bear might have claimed and fed on it during the night, and could be guarding it from a nearby bed. If you find that a bear has been at the scene, consider all options before deciding whether you want to investigate more closely and salvage what's left. Bears can be quite possessive regarding their food.

Most hunters believe that the best animal is the one that falls on the uphill side of the road. Unfortunately, that isn't always the case. Transporting a carcass can be a strenuous ordeal.

In the case of a smallish elk and easy(downhill) terrain, a simple drag technique is common. Merely grab an antler or leg, and pull. One hunter might drag a carcass downhill, but it usually takes two people to drag across rugged terrain or uphill. A big bull will require a small army of men.

Before you drag, look over the options. Consider the terrain, and locations of roads and trails. You might want to drag your animal to a spot that's easier to get to, other than where your vehicle happens to be parked.

If the going is rough and brushy, plan your route carefully. Walk ahead a few yards, determine exactly where you want to go, and pull the carcass to that area. When you reach it, repeat the process until you've made it to your destination.

Dragging is easier if you lift the head off the ground. Sever the front legs at the knee joint, or tie them up around the shoulders; the carcass will slide much easier.

If your quarry lies in a nasty hole or canyon bottom, you might consider returning with a rucksack or packframe, carrying the meat out in boned chunks or quarters.

You can eliminate a surprising amount of weight by boning the carcass and discarding fat, bloodshot areas, the hide, head, and bones. An elk that dresses 500 pounds, for example, will normally yield less than 250 pounds of usable meat.

You don't need to be a certified butcher to bone an animal. Simply cut away large chunks, trimming fat and other unwanted flesh. As you work, lay the meat in cheesecloth, and when you have 10 or 20 pounds in the cloth, tie it tightly and hang it in a nearby tree, allowing it to cool. Keep working until

You must cool an elk carcass quickly, so be sure you have the proper gear to hang it. A block and tackle and sturdy rope are helpful.

the job is done, and fill your pack with as much meat as you can comfortably carry.

Again, be aware of laws governing evidence of sex before you cut away the sex organs.

It might be easier and quicker to carry out the quarters, but the quartering job takes some doing. Start by cutting the animal in half, separating the front from rear quarters. You might want to skin the carcass first, but many hunters leave the skin intact to keep the meat clean.

Cut between the third and fourth ribs, from the brisket to the spine on each side. Then use a saw to cut through the spine, separating both halves.

The tough part is cutting down through the center of the vertebrae, and you'll likely want to trade off with your partner or rest frequently if you're alone. Portable saws work well, but it's always a tedious operation. As you saw, keep the cut centered, otherwise you'll ruin parts of the excellent loin located on each side of the spine.

A quarter from a mature bull elk will weigh 75 to 85 pounds, which is as much as most grown men want to carry. Consider your physical condition, the terrain, and the distance you have to hike before you hoist the load on your back.

Using a horse might appear to be the best way to haul meat, but don't try it unless you are familiar with horses and packing. If you're with an outfitter, he'll tend to the project, but be careful if you rent a horse or use your own horse and are a newcomer to packing game. Two horses are required to pack an elk.

Always assume that your horses are unaccustomed to smelling and seeing a dead animal at close range, unless you know better. Most are, unless they're trained otherwise.

If your horse balks, try this technique, but only if you're savvy to horses. Tie the horse by its halter rope (never the reins) to a tree near the carcass. Gently place a coat over its head, covering its eyes. Scoop up a handful of blood and smear it over the animal's nose. The horse will probably dance and jerk around a bit, but will soon calm down. Keep the horse's head covered while you load the meat, uncovering it when the job is done.

Meat is packed out in halves or quarters. The latter is most common. The easiest way is to pack each quarter in a pannier, which is a box or sturdy canvas bag that hangs on each side of a packsaddle. When you load one pannier, have a companion lift it's weight partially up and off the horse until the opposite pannier is loaded.

Mannying is a more complicated technique. Each quarter is wrapped in a 6x6 or 8x8 foot square sheet of tarp called a manny, and tied directly to a special saddle. This method is complicated and should be done only by experienced hunters. Don't try it unless you know the technique.

Be sure you apply generous amounts of orange flagging to the carcass and horse when you transport game for safety reasons.

A pole-carry works well with a very small elk or for carring quarters or perhaps a half. Find a sturdy pole, lash the meat to the middle, and carry it out with a hunter on each end. An extra shirt bunched under the pole will help pad your shoulders.

One-wheeled carts are showing up all over the West. Most hunters make their own; others buy them from manufacturers. In some areas you can get to a carcass with a snowmobile or all-terrain vehicle. Check the laws governing their use, and respect the presence of other hunters who may be in the area.

Transporting your meat home from your western hunt can be a major problem, but you can eliminate much of the hassle by being prepared.

If you drive, you can tow a small trailer for your meat, or rent a U-Haul in a western town and tow it one way to your home. Be advised, however, that during hunting season, rental trailers are often tough to come by.

If the meat is thoroughly chilled, you can wrap the carcass or each quarter tightly in an old quilt or sleeping bag, and then wrap it again in a tarp. Be sure the sun doesn't hit it as you drive. You'll be amazed at how the meat will stay chilled. The maximum period to keep it wrapped is about two days.

You can also bone the meat or cut it in large chunks and transport it chilled it a well-insulated cooler. Never quickfreeze meat chunks, because you'll have to thaw it to cut it, and then refreeze it, which is never a good idea.

If you have time and can find a meat processor who can butcher the meat and quickfreeze it, you can take it home in insulated cartons. Most wild game processors are extremely busy during hunting season; they might not be able to meet your schedule. If that's the case, they can send the meat to you via a freight company, but it's expensive, usually running $1 to $1.50 per pound for freight charges.

Dry ice will keep meat frozen as long as the ice lasts. You can usually buy it at supermarkets. Ask the clerk how much dry ice you'll need for the amount of meat you have.

If you fly to your western hunt, you can doublewrap the chilled meat tightly in freezer paper, place the packages in a double heavy-duty garbage bag, and place it in a sturdy duffle. Check the meat as baggage, but be sure it doesn't exceed the airline limit of 70 pounds. Most airlines allow you to check three bags. If the meat is extra, you'll be charged an additional fee of around $25 to $35 per bag. If you ship dry ice, you must notify the airline clerk and fill out a special form.

Meat can also be shipped via overnight or two-day air couriers, but the cost is extremely expensive.

In many towns you can trade your meat for salami and sausages. Your meat will be weighed, and you'll be allowed to trade it for an equal amount of already processed meat. You'll also have to pay a quoted price per pound to cover labor, spices, and beef or pork suet that's added. Of course, you don't get your precise meat back in the trade, but quality processors offer excellent foods, and you won't need to worry about quality.

Remember, improper cooling of meat often leads to a "gamey" taste, and can result in spoilage. It's essential to chill the carcass immediately following the kill by prompt field-dressing and proper care afterward.

Aging of meat adds much to its quality, but it must be done properly. The best way to age is to hang the meat in a walk-in cooler, but it can be done outside if the weather cooperates.

If the weather is warm, take it to a meat processing plant if you can't hang it in a cool garage, outbuilding, or basement. If the air temperature is around 50 degrees during the day and cools during the night, skin the animal(if you haven't done so already), and allow it to hang for a few days before taking it to a butcher or cutting it up yourself. If the weather is cooler during the day, the animal can age with the skin on.

There's a special precaution during September hunts. The weather is often very warm — as high as 80 degrees or more. You must act quickly to cool the meat.

To protect the carcass from flies, wrap it entirely within a game bag. If you're hanging quarters, wrap them in individual game bags. Don't wrap them in cheap cheesecloth bags; flies can lay their eggs through them. Some hunters wrap the carcass, but tie it off at the throat. That's a mistake; flies will crawl down the nostrils, into the cavity, and lay eggs.

If you see egg masses deposited by flies, simply scrape them off the meat. You can find them all if you're careful. If you miss some, maggots will begin working in the meat. Cut that portion away and quickly have the meat processed.

A good ol' horse is an elk hunter's best friend, but a horse can be a nightmare if not trained to pack fresh meat. Be sure you know what you're doing before attempting to use a horse.

Cooling a carcass is the primary reason you'd skin it in the field; otherwise you'll do it back in camp or home.

If you skin in the field, be careful to keep dirt away from the carcass. If possible, hang the animal from a tree while it's being skinned. Of course, hanging a mature elk is practically impossible unless you have lots of help and/or a winch or block and tackle.

When skinning the elk on the ground, skin the top side, lay the skin on the ground and roll the carcass on it to keep it off the forest floor; then skin the other side.

Cut or saw the lower legs off at the knee joint. The leg can be cut off with a pocketknife if you know where the joint is; otherwise saw it off. Make a cut from the inside of the knee up the leg along the thigh and to the initial cut you made when field-dressing. Repeat on the other leg. Peel hide away, pulling with one hand and cutting as you go. Cut the tail at the root, and continue to cut and pull downward. Make a slit up the forelegs from the knee to the brisket and peel the hide. As you work, keep hair from getting on the meat. Skin the animal to the throat, and cut the head off at a vertebrae joint, or grab the head and twist it around until it breaks free at a joint.

If you decide to cut up your elk instead of having it commercially done, you'll need a sturdy table to work on, sharp knives, a sharpening stone, pans for meat, freezer paper, tape, and a marking pen.

Don't be concerned if you don't have a bandsaw to cut through bones; you can merely cut around them and discard the bones.

Whether you're working on a spike, cow, or big bull, the procedure is the same, but it will obviously take longer to cut up a larger animal.

Before you start, have four pans available; one each for hamburger meat, stew meat, steaks, and roasts.

Remove the loins from inside the cavity first and cut them into small steaks. Next, cut away the loins from the back and cut them into steaks as well. It's best to wrap the same type steaks in the same package for uniformity. Label each package with the type of cut and date.

The next steps depend on how accurate you want to be, but most hunters simply cut away roasts and steaks from choice sections and make stew meat and burger from areas such as the neck, back, and lower legs. You can rent videos that show how to cut up meat, or read instructions in specialized books.

Burger is the only meat that requires special handling. You can have a butcher do it, or grind it yourself in small specialty grinders that can be purchased from mail order catalogs or hardware stores.

When wrapping meat, consider the size portions you'll need for the number of people who will be eating it.

Generally, steaks and roasts will keep well for about a year in the freezer; stew meat and burger will keep about half that long. To prevent freezer burn, use quality freezer paper.

You might have heard that bull elk are gamey tasting if they're killed during the rut. I've taken about 10 mature bulls during the bugle period — without exception their meat was delicious, and three of those bulls were at least eight years old. Proper aging, marinating, and cooking will eliminate the off-taste if indeed there is any.

Fat from wild game animals must be completely trimmed

away. It is the greatest contributor to strong tasting meat.

There is virtually no piece of edible meat that cannot be cooked by a recipe that will render it delicious. If all else fails, cut tough or gamey meat into chunks and cook it long and slow in a stew pot.

Elk are superb on the table. Make every effort to take care of your meat, from when it hits the ground to when you package it for the freezer.

— Chapter 11 —

Hunting the Wallow

"That bull elk is crazy," my companion whispered. "What in the world is he doing?"

I watched, fascinated, as the animal rolled around and around in a mudhole, kicking mud and filthy brown water in all directions.

"I'm not sure," I said, "but he seems to be enjoying it."

Finally, the six-point bull climbed out and walked off, with a fresh coat of mud glistening on his hide.

That happened more than 20 years ago, when I was new to the West. I had been hunting blue grouse with a pal when the elk's splashing had caught our attention. We had walked over quietly, not knowing what to expect, and had been amazed at the sight.

I hadn't known it at the time, but the bull was behaving normally. As I've since learned, elk commonly wallow in mud during the late summer and early fall.

Biologists believe that elk use wallows for two reasons: to cool themselves, and to perform part of their breeding ritual.

Dr. Valerius Geist of the University of Calgary says that wallowing is done mainly by older bulls, but that wallows also attract yearlings. Geist, considered to be one of the world's top elk authorities, believes that bulls tend to return to the same wallows each year.

Other wildlife experts support Geist's contention that wallows are used primarily by mature bulls, and some scientists feel that the wallow is a mark of advertisement or a dominance display.

According to Geist, a bull will dig a wallow with his front feet, bugling and tearing at the ground with his antlers while digging. At the same time, the bull directs a spray of urine onto the underside of his neck and then rolls about in the wallow after it is dug, continuing to urinate in the wallow. As the bull rolls, he rubs his neck mane on the edge of the wallow and cakes his face, chest, belly, legs and sides with mud.

After wallowing, the bull often rubs his mud-caked neck on the trunk of a nearby tree. He may also thrash saplings and bushes with his antlers, stripping off bark and demolishing branches.

Although elk wallows have been noted by biologists for years, the ritual is not completely understood. Some scientists feel that a single bull will "own" a wallow, and if the bull is killed, another bull will take the wallow over.

According to another belief, the sudden absence of bulls at traditional wallows could indicate a serious reduction in the number of mature bulls in that particular area.

Most biologists believe that wallows are not essential for breeding rituals, pointing to elk areas where there are few, if any, wallows. Those areas, however, are often in lowlands or arid locations where dirt habitat conditions prevent elk from digging wallows.

After watching the bull cavort in the wallow that first time, I began to pay attention to every mudhole and dug-up spot in moist ground that I found. If I hadn't observed the wallowing bull, I'd have continued to ignore those hotspots of elk activity, just as I'd ignored whitetail scrapes in Eastern woods those many years ago.

It's interesting how quickly we're learning about animal behavior. Whitetail scrapes, for example, weren't understood until fairly recently. Early books—classics in their day—on whitetail deer never mentioned scrapes. Now, everyone who hunts whitetails has heard about scrapes, and hunters who correctly utilize scrapes score more consistently than those who don't.

Modern wildlife scientists are unraveling amazing behavior patterns involving big-game species, and hunters are incorporating these discoveries into hunting strategies. Elk wallows are a good example.

It's obvious that hunting near wallows can be an effective technique, but most elk hunters are unaware of the

Bulls love to wallow. Just look at how this old boy is enjoying himself! (Kathy Etling photo).

possibilities. During my big-game hunting lectures each year, I ask the audiences a series of questions to determine their level of elk knowledge. On the question of wallows, many people have no idea of their importance, although most report seeing wallows while hunting.

When I was learning about elk hunting many years ago, an old-timer taught me some valuable lessons. He killed an elk every year, and he took most of them by hunting wallows. Although it might not seem unusual for a skilled hunter to take an elk every year, my friend did it in a state that had a poor elk hunting success rate. A spike bull was cause for celebration in that part of the country, and it would earn admiring glances as it was shown off.

My friend used a simple technique to take his elk back then. He would merely wait for a bull to show up at a beaver pond that had some active wallows and fresh rubs adjacent to it. He told me that most elk appeared during the hottest part of the day—between 2 p.m. and 4 p.m.—and that an early snowstorm or cold front often resulted in little or no elk activity at the wallow.

Because wallowing usually occurs when temperatures are high, bowhunters who try for elk in the late summer can set up stands near active wallows. In states where bow seasons start in August and early September, hunting near wallows is often the only effective technique if bulls aren't responding to calls.

I've observed elk using wallows as early as mid-August. Once, when I was fishing for brook trout in August along a remote creek, I came to a beaver dam and noted fresh elk tracks everywhere. I investigated further, and found a mudhole 25 yards uphill from the dam where a seep moistened the fertile soil. Elk tracks were distinctly imprinted in the bottom of the wallow.

Several hours later, I hiked back down and heard a large animal crash through the timber somewhere near the beaver pond. I didn't see the animal, but the wallow was muddy and freshly disturbed. I'm convinced that I'd spooked a bull elk that had been frolicking in the wallow.

Another time, while bowhunting for deer in late August, I watched a spike bull elk in a wallow. When I spotted him, he was standing in the middle of the wallow and sniffing the edges of the mudhole. He then proceeded to roll in the mud before walking off in the forest.

The wallow was in a limited-entry hunting unit that required a hunter to obtain a tag in a lottery draw. When a friend of mine drew a tag, I took him to the wallow. He killed a fine six-point bull on opening day as the animal was walking down a trail toward the mudhole.

The following year, another pal drew a permit, and it was a repeat performance. He took a big five-point bull on the second day of the season as the bull jumped out of it's bed 75 yards from the wallow. The bull's flanks and mane were caked with mud.

Hunting wallows offers an obvious new dimension to elk hunting. The prime bugling period is generally from mid to late September. Bulls are often silent or only moderately vocal before the rut is in full swing, and they usually won't answer a call at this time. This is when hunting wallows pays off.

Bow seasons are typically held during the rut in the Western states because hunters must get close to their quarry to score. Calling is almost mandatory for elk hunters, but early

This bull just walked into a wallow. Don't overlook these mudholes when you hunt. Bulls are attracted to them in hot weather.

seasons that begin in August offer little opportunity to bugle in a bull. Most elk simply aren't interested. Other than trying to sneak up on a bedded or moving elk, hunting next to a wallow is about the only strategy that will allow a close-in shot.

Stalking close to a herd of elk isn't impossible. In fact, I've found it easier to sneak close to elk than to get near a deer. I suspect the reason for this is that elk are noisy animals because of their large size, and they will tolerate natural noises, such as branches and twigs being broken, that are often made by stalking hunters. Metallic or obviously man-made noises, of course, won't be tolerated. But even though a bowhunter might be able to stalk close, it's another story to thread an arrow into a vital area of a bedded elk. Generally, an elk will be surrounded by brush or trees, and even if a clear shot is possible, the elk's position while bedded often offers a

Since wallows are used during the breeding season, bulls do a lot of talking around them. When you discover a fresh wallow, use your bull and cow call. A bull might assume you're invading his territory. Be on the look out when you blow that call!

very small target area. A hunter using a rifle would have a better chance of scoring, and he wouldn't have to sneak so close.

Watching trails for elk is often an exercise in futility, unless you've found a well-used trail leading to the neck of an active wallow or a trail that's consistently used by elk simply moving from one area to another. Finding one of the latter type of trail, however, is a big order because elk normally travel in small herds over a vast area. You'll be looking for a group of animals in an enormous landscape, and most movement will be withing an hour of sunrise and sundown. This doesn't leave you much time to hunt the trails.

I know several bowhunters who hunt wallows exclusively in August and early September because of the poor odds of stalking bedded or moving elk. Many hunters don't have the luxury of time, and they can't spend days merely walking through a forested area. They concentrate their efforts in high-use areas that attract elk. Wallows fill the bill nicely.

There's another major reason to consider hunting wallows an important strategy: For numerous reasons—including general weather patterns, local storms and heavy hunting pressure—elk will sometimes refuse to bugle or respond to a call, even during the peak of the rut. Many skilled hunters and outfitters believe that today's elk are bugling less than they used to. It's felt that the enormous increase in elk calling by hunters is having an effect on elk behavior. Bulls are getting wise to elk calls, and they are refusing to answer.

No experts believe that elk have completely quit bugling because calling is an important aspect of the breeding ritual. Instead, most feel that calling is now most frequently done at night. I've camped in elk country many times in the past, sleeping in a small mountain tent literally amidst elk herds. Night bugling by elk is routine, but in the past few years I've heard much more nightime vocalization than I had in the past. I believe that this can be attributed to the fact that the area I hunt is public land where elk calling by hunters has increased a great deal in recent years.

Extremely dry, hot weather often has a negative impact on bugling, too, and under these conditions elk tend to become silent, refusing to call or respond to calls. The 1987 season was a good example. Balmy fall days with temperatures in the 80's were common throughout the West, and elk activity seemed to come to a halt. Even in the best elk country, it was tough to hear an elk bugle during the peak of the rut.

What all of this means is that elk bugling can't always be counted on. And when the bulls aren't bugling, wallow hunting offers another ace in the hole when conventional methods won't work.

The next logical question is, how does one find an elk wallow? Unfortunately, there isn't any sure-fire way, but there are some general rules that have the best potential. Wet places are obvious spots. Creek bottoms, especially those dammed by beavers, often are good wallow locations. When you walk the bottoms, crisscross the drainage if you can and look for elk tracks around it, and there may also be a well-used trail leading to it.

A freshly rubbed tree is a good clue to a wallow's presence, too. Investigate the area around the tree closely, even if it means making an out-of-the-way crossing through a marsh or a brushy tangle.

Once when I was hiking along a steep mountain, I stopped in a small clearing and looked across the canyon. With my binoculars, I saw three saplings that had been recently demolished. The bark had been stripped away, leaving naked yellow wood that was easily seen. I guessed that an elk had thrashed the trees, and I hiked over to look. I had to make a difficult crossing through a thick spruce blowdown, and then had to wade the stream at the bottom to get to the rubbed trees.

The trip was worth it, though, as a fresh wallow was located just 10 yards from the trees, and the size of the elk tracks in the area convinced me that the wallow was worthy of special attention. Shooting light was almost over, so I headed for camp, intending to hunt the area in the morning.

As luck would have it, I intercepted a good bull about 500 yards from camp at sunrise the next morning. When I fired at the elk, my pal heard the shot and walked over to help me field-dress and skin the bull. My companion had just left camp and was headed in another direction. Like me, he had discovered an active wallow and had figured on hunting it that day.

When the skinning chore was over, I suggested that my pal hunt the wallow I'd located because it was much closer to camp than the one he'd found. I insisted on quartering the carcass myself because my partner would lose too much hunting time if he stayed to help. As it was, the dressing and skinning job had taken up plenty of time, and there was only a half-day left for him to hunt. He agreed and headed out for the closer wallow.

I had just finished hanging the last quarter when my pal showed up. He was wearing a big grin, and he told me about the six-point elk he'd shot. The animal had been just leaving the wallow with a fresh coat of mud on when my buddy had spotted him.

Wallows are also common along mountainsides where underground springs and seeps emerge. You can spot these areas by noting the different forms of vegetation near the moist areas. Lush grasses and shrubs often grow in wet spots, and

Bulls mark their wallows by rubbing trees. If you see such a tree in the distance, investigate closely...you might discover a fresh wallow!

their foliage is distinctive compared with that of adjacent trees.

Although elk can come to a wallow at any time of day or night, I've found that the late afternoon seems to be a productive time. Most hunters experienced in wallow hunting agree. Bowhunters often either build a tree stand near a wallow or use a portable stand. Hunters using firearms normally find a vantage point within good shooting distance.

Some hunters—myself inculuded—don't have the patience to sit for very long around a wallow, and they prefer instead to still-hunt in the vicinity of a mudhole. Elk country is usually so big that it's tough to cover it thoroughly. Knowing where wallows are helps pinpoint places being used by bulls. In one area I hunt, I know of four active wallows sites in a single drainage. I can visit the wallows in two hours' time if I walk steadily, but I usually spend the entire day just wandering about in the woods and brush around each of them.

Using bull and cow calls around fresh wallows makes good sense—you KNOW elk are using the area.

Elk hunting is tough, and it makes sense to use every strategy you can to turn the odds in your favor. Wallows are foremost in my bag of tricks. The concept works, and that's good enough for me. Anything that puts me closer to a bull elk is worthy of my attention, and wallows do just that.

Chapter 12

A Hunt To Remember

(This chapter was reprinted from OUTDOOR LIFE magazine. The article recounts an amazing experience I had in Canada, in which I took a dandy bull by using a cow call.)

At first, it had looked so easy, but now I was having profound second thoughts. The montain was steeper than I had figured, and the sun was relentless. It wasn't supposed to be this hot in British Columbia during elk season.

Karl Schmidider and I kept climbing, easing our way cautiously up a razorback ridge that led to the mountaintop.

I peeled my shirts off and stuffed them into my daypack. Three hours before, I had shivered while riding a horse up the canyon, but now I was ready to shuck even the soaked T-shirt that clung to my skin.

It had been my idea to tie the horses and climb the mountain. There had been no special reason to do so, except to see what was on the other side. Our luck had been so bad that we were game for anything.

When we reached the summit, I lay down in the shade of a bush. Karl did likewise, and we relaxed as a freshening breeze occasionally wafted along and cooled the hot air.

If only Karl or I had had the good sense to carry a canteen, we would have been in better spirits. As it was, we cussed ourselves for our forgetfulness. The creek's soft gurgle far down in the canyon bottom didn't help, either. We were intensely thirsty. The air temperature was close to 90 degrees, and we had been climbing steadily for two hours.

I lay there with my head on my daypack, thinking about

my parched mouth, when I noticed a large can on the ground several yards away.

"What's that big can doing up here in the middle of nowhere?" I asked Karl.

"Probably from Henry's sheep cache," Karl answered without moving. "This is where he sets up one of his spike camps."

Suddenly, Karl sat up and looked. Instantly, he was on his feet, and then I heard him grumble in his thick German accent. I vaguely made out a few choice unprintable words and something about grizzly bears.

I walked over to Karl, and saw the mess on the ridgetop. Cans, bottles and all sorts of food containers were scattered for 50 yards. A large metal drum—its contents gone—was lodged in some brush down the slope.

Karl pointed to the heavy stainless-steel cables that had once held the drum. The grizzly had not only ripped the drum from its cable moorings, but had also slashed open the heavy metal top, which had been tightly sealed.

Looking over the assortment of containers, I spotted a can of peaches still intact. I picked it up and immediately opened it with my knife. Karl declined my offer to share the peaches, but rummaged around and came up with a jug of water and more cans of fruit.

To the victor go the spoils, I thought, feeling like a coyote that cleans up on a grizzly kill. We indulged in the find, and later picked up most of the garbage and tossed it back into the drum.

"Henry will not be happy," Karl said, "but the bears are boss."

It was a simple statement, and having spent a great deal of time in grizzly country, I agreed.

With our thirst quenched, we lay down again, making small talk about bears, Canadians, Americans, world problems, women's rights and, naturally, elk hunting.

Karl, a German immigrant to Canada, guides for outfitter Henry Fercho in southeastern British Columbia's Kootenay Mountains. Karl and I had hit it off immediately, forming a great relationship between hunter and guide. We understood each other perfectly, and I genuinely enjoyed his company. He was about 10 years older than I, and I liked his old-world European values and philosophy of life. Hunting with him was a pleasure, even though the weather had so far turned our elk efforts into futile ones.

The hunt had been organized by Bushnell/Bausch & Lomb to evaluate some new binoculars and riflescopes. Our party was made up of nine hunters, including General Chuck Yeager, former astronaut Joe Engle and hunting consultant Jack Atcheson, who had arranged the hunt. Henry had split us into three groups, with three hunters in each group. Mine included Yeager and Don Robertson, an executive with Bushnell.

Although we were hunting in September during the prime bugling season, the elk weren't cooperating because of the intense heat and extremely dry weather. I'd seen this happen before during hot weather, and wasn't surprised. Although elk will go about their breeding as usual under these conditions, they're far less vocal and less likely to respond to calling.

Neither Don, Chuck nor I had heard an elk bugle during the first three days, though we had hunted hard and had never seen camp in the daylight. On the first day, Yeager had killed a black bear with an unbelieveable single shot at 450 yards. More than anything, he had wanted to give his first grandson a bear rug for Christmas. The salted bear pelt in camp had given us all a bit of encouragement.

We now walked off the steep mountain to our horses, and Karl figured that it would be a good idea to hunt the higher country. (Henry has more than a dozen elk camps in his vast hunting unit—all are very comfortable cabins accessible by horses.) We headed back to camp to have a "round table" with the other guides.

Yeager, Robertson and their guides rode into camp during midday. After a brief discussion, there was a unanimous decision to move up to a camp in a glacial cirque. When we learned that a fine mountain lake loaded with cutthroat trout was just a few yards from the cabin, Yeager's eyes lit up.

"Let's go," he said. "I just happen to have a pack rod in my duffel. We can share it."

After we packed our gear, Yeager and I stood near the cabin and talked about elk. Suddenly, a gust of wind blew through the trees, shaking hundreds of brilliantly hued aspen leaves from their branches.

"What a beautiful sight," Yeager said as the bright leaves spun delicately to the forest floor. "That's what hunting is all about. Just seeing the natural beauty in this wilderness is worth it."

This was not my first trip with Chuck Yeager, so his eloquent remarks didn't surprise me. But to many people who know Yeager as a tough, fearless fighter pilot who knocked down five German warplanes in one day, or as a test pilot who still flies brand-new jets, or as a retired general who is a former director of safety for the U.S. Air Force, those comments would perhaps have raised a few eyebrows.

The truth is that Chuck Yeager was all of the above at one time or another, and through it all, he has never lost his intense love of the outdoors no matter where in the world he has traveled. After a half-dozen hunting and fishing trips with Yeager, I know him as one of the most ardent, avid outdoorsmen I have ever been acquainted with.

In addition, the man is good. Whether he's casting a dry fly for a cagey rainbow trout, or hitting a squirrel in the eye with a .22 bullet, or skillfully battling a 50-pound king salmon, he's good.

Yeager says that one of the reasons why he survived World War II was because of the woodlore skills he had learned while growing up in rural West Virginia. When his airplane was shot down over German-occupied France, he managed to escape through snowy mountains while dragging a wounded buddy. Yeager's oldest son, Don, told me of several close calls in Vietnam when he had survived only because his dad had taught him how to live in the outdoors.

As we rode along the trail to the higher elk camp, a grouse jumped up on a log and eyed us curiously. Yeager dismounted immediately and looked for rocks on the ground. We all knew his intentions when we saw the slingshot. Two minutes and four shots later, Yeager walked back to the trail with four grouse in his hand.

"Here's dinner, boys," He said with a wide grin. "Now, let's catch some trout to go with the birds."

We had barely arrived in camp when Yeager rushed to the

Chuck Yeager displays proof of his hunting talents while hunting elk with Jim Zumbo...Four grouse with four shots from his slingshot!

lake with his rod and assortment of shrimp-pattern flies that had been tied by his son, Mickey. A half-hour later, he returned to the cabin and handed me his Loomis rod.

"Your turn," he said. "I'll clean these fish, and you bring me some more."

I wasted no time getting to the water. I was eager to add some trout to the frying pan, but I was also anxious to have a general clean my fish. At that moment, elk hunting was far from top priority.

We had a splendid dinner that evening and talked about the new stategy for the morning, which was to walk from the cabin to prime areas and try bugling.

But despite our efforts the next day, the elk didn't respond favorably. We all heard bulls bugle, but the animals were entrenched in extremely dense timber. No matter what we tried, the bulls were uninterested.

Other animals, however, kept us amused while the elk were uncooperative. We saw plenty of bighorn sheep, moose and both black and grizzly bears. One afternoon, Karl and I saw six black bears and a grizzly feeding on a slope that was blanketed with lush berry patches. Though I had a black bear tag, I didn't intend to try for a bear until I had first taken a bull elk.

Karl and I did work a bull in a basin on the seventh and eighth mornings, but the bull bugled a dozen times or so before eventually melting farther into the forest.

When the same bull answered our call on the ninth morning, I suggested to Karl that we try something different. I left Karl at our vantage point to continue bugling occasionally while I eased about 150 yards down the slope.

I found a good position and blew a cow call. By that time, the bull had quit responding to Karl's bugle, as he'd done the previous two mornings. When there was no answer to my call, I waited five minutes and blew it again. Still, there was no answer, so I waited ten minutes and tried once more. After giving the bull another 10 minutes, I decided that he wasn't going to show, and climbed back up the mountain toward Karl.

I was about 10 yards from Karl when he pointed down into the basin. I turned to see a respectable six-point bull silently walking toward my former position. Cussing myself for

General Yeager tends to his horse before trekking into British Columbia's wilderness country.

leaving, I made a quick decision after studying the bull. The wind had begun to swirl, and the bull had changed his direction of travel, heading back into the timber from where he had come.

The shot would be around 350 yards. Had I stayed where I was when I had used the cow call, the bull would have been only 200 yards out.

But there was no time to lament. I found a solid rest for my .30/06, and figured the elevation for that distance. I didn't like having to shoot that far, but I was confident in my rifle as well as the new 2.5X-to-10X Bausch & Lomb scope that topped it.

The elk was standing broadside at the first shot, and I knew that the bullet had hit low. Instead of running, however, the bull took a step and looked around, confused by the echo of the shot in the basin. The next shot was also low, and the bull walked rapidly toward a pocket of heavy timber. Now, I was upset with myself because I was questioning my rifle's performance. At that point, though, I realized that the bull was probably much farther away than I'd originally figured. The elk slowed momentarily to step over a log, and I raised the

There are lots of pleasurable moments during an elk hunt, like relaxing around camp during the day when the temperature is too hot for effective hunting.

crosshairs a full 14 inches. At the shot, the bull faltered momentarily and ran into the timber.

Sitting quietly after the last shot, I heard a thump in the forest that sounded like a big animal falling heavily to the ground. The wind had been perfectly calm at that point, enabling me to hear for a long distance.

I was confident that I'd hit the elk, but Karl wasn't so sure. He hadn't seen the elk when I'd shot the third time, and he hadn't heard the thump because he had been walking through brush down toward me.

"Long shot," Karl said, almost apologetically.

"Real long," I answered. "A lot farther than I figured, but I believe he's down."

With no further discussion, we worked our way down to

where the bull had stood when I had shot at him. I found the exact spot where the elk had been stepping when I'd fired, but found no trace of blood. There was a set of deep hoofprints where the bull had lunged after the shot, but the dry ground revealed no more tracks.

Karl and I searched for a full hour in vain. There was not a speck of blood, and I was starting to lose my former confidence.

"You really think you hit him?" Karl asked.

"I don't know what to think," I answered. "I was sure I heard him fall, and I saw him stagger when I shot, but now I'm not at all sure."

We searched some more, but still found no evidence of the blood or hair that would signify a hit.

What happened next still makes me shudder when I think about it.

"I don't think he's hit," Karl said, "but we'll keep on looking if you want to."

"I'm beginning to think you're right," I said. "Let's try once more, and then head for camp if we don't find anything."

Again we looked, this time covering more area in the very dense forest. We made large circles, moving slowly and calling out to each other so that we could look methodically.

Finally, when it seemed that we had done everything humanly possible to find the elk, I convinced myself that I'd missed. I'd crawled around on my hands and knees so much, looking for the tiniest pinhead of blood, that my knees ached.

"Let's go," I said. "I missed."

As I turned to leave, I wondered what Chuck Yeager would think back at camp. It's no sin to miss, after all, and I had done it before, but I felt as though I'd let Karl, Henry, the Bushnell people and the rest of our party down.

But as we were climbing out of the basin, I had a powerful sense of recall that made me stop in my tracks. In my mind, I reenacted the precise moment of the shot, and I clearly saw the elk falter. He hadn't simply slipped or stumbled—he had reacted to the impact of the bullet. Just as clearly, I heard the thump over and over.

Suddenly, I knew that the elk was dead. There was no question about it.

"I'll meet you back at camp, Karl," I said. "I want to try one more time.

Karl looked at me incredulously. "I'll go with you," he said.

"It will only take me a few minutes," I answered. "That bull is dead. Wait here, and I'll call you."

I ran back down the mountain like a crazy man. It mattered no longer that there was no blood. This had happened to me before, even while bowhunting and making a fatal hit with an arrow. Blood doesn't have to be present.

When I reached the area, I walked confidently to the spot where I had seen the bull falter—the same spot that Karl and I had searched several times. A strange force was guiding me onward. I felt goose bumps crawling around on the back of my neck and my arms, and I knew the elk was close.

Incredibly, I spotted the bull lying in a small gully that was surrounded by a tight cluster of spruce trees. He'd lunged into a depression that had contained his body perfectly, and he had died with his belly to the ground, his back to the sky and his legs folded beneath him. His hair blended perfectly with the sun-dappled underbrush, and his antlers were shrouded by low branches of thick spruces.

I waited a moment before calling Karl, as I was overwhelmed with emotion, reflecting on the tragedy that had almost occurred.

Karl and I field-dressed the bull, and I noted that the Remington Core-Lokt bullet had penetrated the bottom half of each lung. The elk had run 85 yards from where I had hit him.

Chuck Yeager returned with Karl and me and the other two guides later that afternoon to pack out the bull. When I showed Yeager where the bull had stood when I had hit him and the mountain slope from where I had fired, he let out a low whistle. "No wonder you shot three times," he said, smiling. "You must have been zeroing in on that bull artillery fashion. If you'd been using my .300 Weatherby Mag, you'd have dropped that old boy in his tracks."

Yeager had a twinkle in his eye as we walked to the bull.

As we approached the elk, Yeager broke off the end of a spruce twig that was shaped like a cross. He dipped it in the elk's blood and then grasped my hand in a firm handshake. Yeager spoke in German and told me what to say in response.

Fishing is always a bonus in elk country. Be sure you bring along a rod if fishing is an option.

I repeated after him, and he translated afterward, explaining that the ceremony was a ritual performed in Germany to show reverence to the elk as well as to the hunter.

I was moved by Yeager's genuine respect for the dead bull. The jet pilot had a lot of class, as well as affection and reverence for wild things.

Yeager left our party early, heading for camp at a trot. I wondered why he had left so soon, but I found out why later.

Just before dinner, everyone in our group was gathered outside the cabin, and I noted some whispering here and there. Yeager walked up to me with a grin on his face and held out his .300 Weatherby Magnum.

"If you'll retire Bertha," he said, "you can have this rifle."

I looked at Bertha, my Winchester Model 70 that I had hunted with faithfully for 25 years, and looked back at Yeager.

Jim Zumbo with the bull that he almost lost. This hunt was a sobering experience. Be sure to follow up every time you shoot -- no matter what the circumstances.

I was dumbfounded—at a loss for words—which is unusual for me.

"Are you serious?" I replied.

Yeager nodded, the grin even wider.

"Suppose I don't retire her, but give her to my son?" I asked. I had been considering that possibility for the last couple of years, anyway.

"It's a deal," Yeager responded. "Next time you shoot at an elk 400 yards away, use this .300. Here's what it did at 200 yards when you were packing out the bull."

Yeager showed me a paper plate with three holes punched neatly in the middle. He had left us and the bull early so that he could make sure the rifle was dead on before giving it to me.

Last Christmas, my son, Danny, opened up a long box to

see a well-used Winchester with a red ribbon tied around the barrel. He looked at me and didn't have to say a word to show his love and gratitude.

As we hugged, I recalled fond memories when Danny had traipsed after me dozens of times as I hunted with Bertha. He had been at my side on many occasions when I had taken deer, elk and antelope with the old rifle, and I remembered when, at age 12, Danny had fired the .30/06 for the first time. It had been a milestone, and I had seen how proud he had been as he blew at the blue smoke curling from the barrel.

When Danny graduated from college last June, we were saying our goodbyes before he headed off to California, where he'd start a new job with McDonnell Douglas in aerospace technology.

"By the way, Dad," he said, "forgot to tell you, but I was varmint hunting with Bertha last week. Shot three rockchucks at 300 yards each, and all in the head."

The kid really knew how to hurt a guy. I smiled as valiantly as I could, all the time mentally thanking Chuck Yeager for giving me the reason to share Bertha with my boy.

Next year, by the way, Danny and I will be hunting together in Wyoming. Bertha still has plenty of straight shots left in her, and when Danny kills his bull, I'm going to look for a spruce twig shaped like a cross and teach him a wonderful custom that I learned high on a mountain in British Columbia.

Thanks again, Chuck.

Notes

Chapter 13

Planning Your Elk Hunt

Planning an elk hunt is a tough assignment. Dozens of questions must be asked and answered before you head out on your trip. For starters, you must make basic decisions — what states to consider, do you hire a guide, will you hunt on your own, exactly where will you hunt, how will you get your game to the road or vehicle (an elk requires major work or planning to transport it through the woods), and how will you eventually get your meat home? These are just a few topics that must be addressed. It makes sense that the better prepared you are, the better odds of success on your hunt.

What State

Unlike mankind, all states were not created equal when it comes to hunting. Each has varying politics and game departments. Elk populations are managed according to the objectives of each wildlife agency, and hunting success rates, as well as the abundance of trophy animals, often reflect those objectives.

As an example, let's compare two states for elk: Colorado and Wyoming. Colorado offers unlimited tags to residents and nonresidents, but Wyoming provides only 8,000 nonresident tags on a lottery draw. Colorado has more elk than Wyoming, but the much heavier hunting pressure in Colorado affords a more consistent harvest of bulls. As a result, Wyoming produces bigger bulls on a comparative basis. A trophy hunter might consider Wyoming, but a hunter who wants to see plenty of elk should look to Colorado, but he should be prepared to see few old, mature bulls in areas of heavy hunter concentrations.

License availability is another important consideration

when selecting a state. Obviously, if you're unsuccessfull in drawing a lottery tag or are too late in a first-come first-served system, you'll hunt a state that offers unlimited tags.

During the planning process, write each state for applications as soon as you decide to hunt the West. Don't delay, because you might miss deadlines. Read the application carefully. Many are complicated, and if you leave out an item of information or forget your signature, the application will be voided.

Should You Hire An Outfitter?

If you hunt certain areas, you might have no choice in hiring an outfitter. In Wyoming, for example, nonresidents may not hunt wilderness areas without a licensed guide.

There are good reasons why you should — and shouldn't hire an outfitter. Cost is a major disadvantage if you're looking to a low-cost economy trip, although you might save in the long run if your economy trip, or a succession of them, end up as failures. The price of an outfitted hunt might have resulted in a savings if you were successful on your first hunt because of his services.

Be aware that elk are difficult to transport. In some regions, an outfitters services are almost mandatory. Unless you're highly prepared with good horses and gear, a wilderness hunt is out of the question on your own.

Access to good elk country is a chief reason for hiring an outfitter, as well as his ability to show you game. He might hunt you on a private ranch via four-wheel drive vehicles, or take you far back into public areas on a horse.

His responsibilities, besides guiding, are to offer basic comforts. He'll feed you, provide sleeping quarters, a sanitary facility, and transport your elk out of camp to a designated area. You are required to bring your own rifle, sleeping bag, and personal gear.

Don't consider an outfitted hunt to be easier than a hunt on your own. In fact, it can be just the opposite. Remember that you'll be following a guide who will likely be tough and conditioned to handle the rigors of the hunt. Besides keeping up with him, you'll rise early in the morning, put in a long day,

Planning a hunt requires lots of homework. Look over updated maps before you go. The more preparation you do, the better.

and fall exhausted into your sleeping bag at night.

Your outfitter won't be able to guarantee you an animal, which might make you think twice before hiring him. You aren't buying an elk; you're buying a hunting opportunity. Too many variables can stymie a hunt, no matter how good the outfitter's reputation or the country he hunts.

Your biggest decision, once you decide to hire an outfitter, is how to find the "right" ones. Back pages of outdoor magazines have dozens of ads, and you can write for a list provided by outfitter associations in individual states. (These offices change frequently; write or call the state wildlife agency for an updated address.) You can also meet outfitters at outdoor expo shows, or buy a trip through a booking agent.

The latter option is the least risky provided the agent is reputable and books only quality, honest outfitters. There are booking agents coming out of the woodwork these days; be careful when you deal with one. For best results, contact a well-established agent who has been in business for a number of years. Your hunt won't cost any more by working through an agent. He works like a travel agent; in this case the outfitter pays his commission. You pay the same price if you deal directly with the outfitter.

Hiring an outfitter yourself requires caution. Most are credible, but some are not. Carefully investigate his operation. Ask for references, but don't write them. You'll get more accurate information on the telephone. Ask them about elk availability, how skillful the guides were, camp conditions, and other pertinent questions. An outfitter will give you a list of references who are satisfied customers — go one step further and ask references for the names and phone numbers of other hunters who shared their camp. You'll get a better feel for the entire operation, and won't have a biased list to work from.

If you hire an outfitter, he'll usually give you a list of gear to bring. A warm sleeping bag is a must, unless you're in a heated building. Tents with woodburning stoves have a way of quickly cooling off when the fire goes out in the middle of the night. A foam pad is a good idea if you're sleeping on cots. Regardless of the quality of your bag, when it's compressed under your weight it will lose its ability to keep you warm. Ask the outfitter prior to the trip if he provides sleeping pads. Personal gear should be carefully considered, again using the outfitter's advice. Never pack it in a suitcase if it will be transported to camp on a horse; use a sturdy duffle bag which is much more easily packed. The outfitter might suggest a maximum weight allowed per hunter — never exceed that weight. (See Chapter 14 for specific hunting and personal items to bring.)

Prior to actually booking the hunt, make sure the outfitter has spelled out all the details. He should give you an accurate description of the hunt's requirements. You should know in advance if strenuous climbing is required, how much horseback riding is involved, and how many days you'll actually be hunting. A seven day hunt, for example, can really mean one day's ride to camp, five days of hunting, and a day's ride out.

By the same token, the oufitter should be aware of your physical condition so he can design your hunting plans accordingly. Don't enlighten him about a serious ailment or shortcoming when you arrive in camp.

Hunting On Your Own

Most hunters will put a trip together with one or more companions, and take their chances on a do-it-yourself hunt. There are some important considerations before planning this project, so be as thorough as possible before you head West.

Knowing precisely were to hunt is a major factor. The best option is to talk to a pal who has been to the area. He can steer you in the right direction and provide valuable information as to where to hunt, camp, etc.

If you make the trip cold, you'll have your work cut out for you. There are plenty of unforeseen risks when you head to an unfamiliar place.

Your first requirement is to write for hunting regulations. Don't delay, because deadlines and application procedures vary in each state. (The address and phone number of each western state wildlife agency is listed in the Appendix of this book).

Next, you need good maps. Assuming you'll be hunting public land, write to the agency that manages the land you'll be hunting. (Check the list of federal agencies in the Appendix).

Two federal agencies manage the bulk of the acreage in the West. The U.S. Forest Service, an agency within the Department of Agriculture, administers land on 101 National Forests in the West. The Bureau of Land Management, a U.S. Department of the Interior agency, also manages enormous amounts of land throughout the West. Generally, national forests are in higher elevations, and were established by Congress for timber production. BLM lands are in lower elevations, and though considered to be a grazing agency, support prime big game habitat on much of its holdings.

Once determining an area you want to hunt, look over the maps carefully. Federal maps will usually show general ownership patterns as well as major and secondary roads. Look for campsites near the hunt area, as well as general access routes. Try to select a primary camp spot and pick a backup as well. It's possible that the campground will be full when you get there, or it might have some shortcomings that you hadn't anticipated.

Once you've focused in on a particular spot, it's a wise idea to order topographic maps. These have much larger scales and show features that aren't on federal maps. Trails, old roads, swamps, springs, and contours are among the very important features you need to be familiar with. To order topographic maps, write to the U.S. Geological Survey, Box 25046, Federal Center, Denver, CO 80225. Ask for an index on your initial request, and then order the specific topo maps you want by referring to the index.

Drop Camps

Here's an economical way to use an outfitter's services while hunting on your own. A drop camp is just that — an outfitter packs you and your gear to one of his camps and drops you off. He'll return at a designated date and pack you and your gear (and game) back out. Rates for drop camps are much less than for fully guided hunts, often 50 to 70 percent lower.

This sounds like a wonderful opportunity, but there are some important drawbacks. First, most outfitters have a prime hunting area that they hunt with their top-paying clients. Obviously, they won't put you in those areas because they don't want you competing with those clients. Second, they're reluctant to place you in prime country because it's possible that you'll show up another year on your own, after learning the country at his expense.

Nonetheless, there are some very good drop camps around. You need to do your homework (by checking references), and determining if it's a good deal.

The standard drop camp has the basic comforts. Normally there should be a sleeping tent and cooking tent. Firewood, cooking utensils, stoves, lanterns, and other camp gear may or may not be available. In some cases, an outfitter might provide a wrangler and horses for your use.

A disadvantage of drop camps is the need to cook, wash dishes, do camp chores, and figure out where to hunt. Many folks enjoy that sort of challenge, however, and like the idea of hunting without being constantly led by a guide. The price is right, too, but before you make hasty plans to book a drop camp, check it out well. It could end up being a nightmare rather than a pleasant hunt.

Scouting is always a good idea. If you can't look over the country before the hunt, discuss a plan with your pals and learn the country. If nothing else, determine the most likely escape areas for elk. Hunt them hard after the season opens.

Applying for Permits

Each state has a unique system of offering elk permits. In practically every state, resident and nonresident tags are not offered in the same manner. Residents are generally preferred, and in the case of many species, 10 percent of the tags go to nonresidents; the rest go to residents.

States that have unlimited tags often require hunters to purchase tags prior to the opener. A few states allow tags to be issued after the season opens, so be sure you're certain of the regulations. You don't want to show up for the hunt and learn that the deadline for purchasing tags is past. Don't rely on information from friends. They might be wrong, and regulations change frequently. Get updated, official information from the state wildlife agency.

Don't gamble with the postal system when deadlines approach. Get your application in well before the due date. Some states require the application to be postmarked by a certain date, while others require the application to be received by a specific date.

Be sure to carefully read the instructions, because most applications are complicated. If you make a simple mistake, your form will be rejected. Wildlife departments have no sympathy for faulty applications.

A common error is to send a personal check along with the application. Your form will be immediately rejected; with rare exceptions, all states require a cashier's check or bank or postal money order.

In the case of states or species that require a lottery draw, most states offer party permits. Several hunters can apply on the same application. You all draw, or no one draws. Be aware that no western states allow party hunting, where a single tag can be shared by more than one hunter. This is common in several eastern states, but in the West the rules are strict. Each hunter harvests his own animal.

You cannot hunt unless you have a tag. Pay attention to details, or this basic step could cost you a hunt if you make a careless mistake.

Limited Entry Hunts

If you want to improve your chances of success and have a much more enjoyable hunt, consider the limited entry hunt. As the name implies, this hunt places a restriction on the number of hunters.

Since hunting pressure is obviously lower, there is less competition. You'll see fewer hunters, hear fewer shots, and have a quality experience.

Because of the lighter pressure, the quarry will have a better chance of survival. By living longer, they grow larger antlers. It's as simple as that.

Most limited entry hunts are on public lands, and access is usually good. You can put together a hunt on your own or with pals, provided you all draw a tag.

Hunter success rates on limited entry areas is consistently higher than on general hunt units, often 20 percent to 50 percent or more. Every state offers these special units. Investigate them carefully, because they offer superb odds of success as well as a less competitive hunt.

Jim Zumbo took this bull after learning the legal boundaries of the hunting unit, as well as the general topography and vegetative types. To hunt elk successfully, it's essential to know their backyard. Doing so will help your odds!

Scouting

Few hunters take the time to scout game country prior to the hunt, and fewer still know how to scout correctly. Because of time limitations, it's tough to squeeze a day or two in before the hunt just to scout. If there are extra days, most hunters will take them during the hunt itself. That's reasonable, but it indicates how unimportant scouting is considered to be.

Luck plays a large part in hunting, but hunters who consistently score do so because they're familiar with the country in which they hunt. Since the West offers hunting on a much larger scale than other regions, it's vital to learn the landscape.

Scouting doesn't mean merely looking for fresh sign or game itself. It goes far beyond that. To understand, let's consider a typical scenario.

Imagine that you're off on a Colorado elk hunt, and you've located a herd of elk the day before the opener. You go to bed excited, and can hardly wait for shooting light. The next morning, however, is not a good day in your book of memories. Several other people also spotted the elk, and the animals are either spooked prematurely by careless hunters, or someone else claims the only bull in the herd.

If you had located fresh sign prior to the opener and planned on hunting it, you might also have scouted in vain. The presence of hunters before the opener and during the first day could cause animals to restructure their behavior patterns. They might not return to the area in which you initially saw fresh sign for several weeks.

Proper scouting involves not only looking for sign or animals, but learning the character of the area. A priority objective is to determine where those elk might go once they're disturbed. Look for dense blowdowns, thick stands of timber, and other areas where spooked elk will seek solitude.

It's just as important to determine their escape areas as it is to learn where they're living prior to the hunt, particularly in areas that are heavily hunted. In places where pressure is light, you can spend more time looking for animals in their routine habitats. Otherwise, go the extra mile and consider where those disturbed animals will go to survive. If you do, you'll be far ahead of the game.

— Chapter 14 —

What To Bring

Gearing up for a western hunt depends on a number of factors, including weather, the type of terrain you'll hunt, whether you hunt on your own or with an outfitter, how you'll get your meat home, and other considerations.

Obviously, a Wyoming bowhunt in 90- degree temperatures will require different gear than a late November Montana hunt with the thermometer reading zero or lower.

If you're a nonresident, a western hunt will require much more gear than a hunt in your state. You'll be travelling a much longer distance, and you'll no doubt be spending much more time on your hunt than on a local foray.

Proper preparation will insure that you'll be comfortable on your hunt. If you're comfortable you'll hunt in a more positive manner, and you'll be a better hunter.

Camp Gear

This is an important matter, one that you must carefully consider. The easiest way to camp is to haul a camp trailer or pickup camper. Your temporary home is self-contained, and you won't need to worry much about weather. A motorhome is questionable, unless you address two important items. First, you must never drive it off secondary roads because of the possibility of getting it stuck in a bad spot. This requirement precludes the possibility of getting close to good game country. Second, you should tow a hunting vehicle with your motorhome, or you won't be mobile. It's vital to have a trustworthy means of transportation.

A tent has always been a basic camp item, and probably always will be. Though a tent doesn't offer all the services that

This Starcraft tent-camper unit is an example of a mobile camp that is economical to tow and easily manuvered in forested campsites. This unit is Jim Zumbo's choice for a base elk camp when he isn't packing into remote areas. (Photo courtesy of Starcraft.)

a hard-sided unit does, it takes up little space and can be erected almost anywhere. Various heat systems keep tent interiors warm and toasty.

Your tent must be waterproof. In most cases, you must waterproof a new tent yourself, regardless of the manufacturer's claims. A tube of sealant should come with your new tent. Apply it to all the seams and every stitch. Erect the tent before the hunt and test it. If it doesn't rain, set a lawn sprinkler so it thoroughly sprays the tent for several hours. This might seem like an unnecessary exercise, but you'll regret it if your hunt is ruined by a wet camp. Nothing dampens spirits quicker than an outdoor adventure where you can't get your clothes dry.

Canvas tents are still popular, but most of them leak where you touch them. For extra protection, apply a layer of plastic or visquine over the roof and secure it tightly so the wind doesn't tear it off.

Your tent should have a floor. If not, use a tarp or piece of plastic. Either could get damp, but at least you'll be free of dirt.

Sleeping cots will provide much more comfort as opposed to sleeping on an air mattress or directly on the ground. Air mattresses sometimes leak, and they're so small you often roll off during the night. A cot has a small amount of sag and tends to hold you securely. Be sure you put a foam pad on the cot. It provides more cushion, but it also keeps you a great deal warmer. Your sleeping bag will compress below you, providing no loft, and you'll be cold and miserable, even in a quality bag if you lie on a cot without a pad.

If you're camping in cold country, a heater will be a nice addition. You can use a wood stove that is collapsible and is transported easily, or you can fire up a kerosene stove. The latter will take the chill out of your tent, but if it's really cold, the wood stove is tops for yielding maximum heat. Catalytic heaters are widely used, but they're not effective if it's windy and bitterly cold. Whatever method of heating you use, be sure there's adequate ventilation, whether you're in a tent or camp unit.

Firewood will be necessary if you heat with a wood stove. Bring along sharp tools. A small chain saw saves time, and be aware of regulations regarding firewood cutting. A permit from the land agency might be required.

Some kind of lighting is required. Flashlights are fine for small chores, but you should have a central unit that provides good illumination. Lanterns are standard, and are fueled by a disposable propane tank or white gas. Be sure you have more fuel than you think you'll need, and bring along a supply of mantles. Wooden matches are best to light the mantles because the flame source must be pushed up through a slot, and larger matches work best.

Sleeping Gear

If you hunt out of a lodge, motel, or boarding house, you might have the luxury of sheets and blankets. It's more likely, however, that you'll be snuggled in a sleeping bag.

Down bags are expensive and will keep you warm during very cold temperatures. Be aware, however, that there are various grades of down. Some sleeping bags are filled with

Having proper gear is a vital consideration. Jim Zumbo looks half-frozen (and he is), but his warm clothing allowed him to hunt elk during the worst conditions. Remember a basic adage -- you can't kill an elk unless you're out there in elk country. Prepare for bad weather!

duck feathers or have only a certain percentage of down. Goose down is the premier filler, and is the most expensive. The label on the bag should identify the kind of down and how many ounces are in the bag.

For all its warmth, down is worthless if it gets wet. The bag will be clammy and cold, and it will take forever to dry.

Synthetic fillers, on the other hand, are easily dried and will retain heat even when wet. They're not as expensive as down, but will keep you just as warm. When shopping for one, check their rating. Some will keep you warm at 15 degrees, some at zero, and some even lower. The amount of loft is a good indicator of the bag's quality. More loft means more heat retention capabilities.

Don't be fooled if you'll be sleeping in a tent warmed by a wood stove, which is likely the case on an elk hunt or any backcountry hunt. You can count on the fire going out during the night, and you'll suffer in an inferior bag.

When packing your sleeping bag, make sure it's in a waterproof container if you're packing in on a horse. It could get wet during the packing operation or on the ride in. An easy way to protect the bag is to simply seal it tightly in two or three heavy-duty garbage bags.

As indicated in the section above on gear, bring a foam pad if you sleep on a cot. No matter how good your bag, your weight will compress it beneath you and you'll lose the warmth qualities. The cold air beneath your cot will quickly chill you where your body contacts the cot's surface. If you forget a pad, place several layers of soft clothing on the cot and sleep on it. The clothing will add more insulation between the sleeping bag and the cot.

Clothing

Western weather can be unpredictable in the fall. Regardless of the long-term forecast, you must be prepared for the worst. Rain, snow, strong winds, and hot days can cause you unforseen hardships.

Generally, you can expect fairly balmy weather in lower elevations during September and October. Rain and snow are always possible, so bring woolen apparel. Wool will keep you warm even when it's wet. High country hunts, no matter what

Most hunters don't have the gear required to transport elk out of the backcountry. In many areas, you can rent horses, but be sure you're savvy to horses and their whims.

the month, are seldom balmy for extended periods. Again, wool is the best answer.

If you're hunting in warm weather, wear comfortable trousers and light shirts. A couple of flannel or cotton shirts over an undershirt will get you by. If the temperature heats up or you start to perspire, remove a shirt and stuff it in your daypack, which you should ALWAYS carry. A heavy woolen shirt and gloves stored in your daypack will be most welcome if a cold front moves in. Be aware that the temperature can easily drop 40 degrees or more in a matter of hours when a storm approaches.

For footwear, a pair of cotton socks inside lightweight, waterproof boots are adequate in warm weather.

When weather turns nasty, polypropylene longjohns topped by warm trousers, one or two wool shirts, a down vest, and a woolen jacket should keep you comfortable. Two pair of wool socks, or a pair of woolen socks over cotton socks will be sufficient foot protection. Insulated, waterproof boots are a must if you're walking in snow. A good pair of gloves will be highly appreciated in cold temperatures. Polypropylene liners inside quality leather gloves are a good combination. Pay attention to your head. A warm hat should protect your ears. The old axiom: "if your feet are cold, put on your hat," is true. You lose a great deal of heat through your head.

Bring along a pair of moccasins or slippers to lounge around in. When you take your boots off after a hard day's hunting, slippers will be a luxury.

Hunter orange clothing is required in many western states. Some rules require a minimum number of square inches. Be sure you're aware of the regulations, and invest in a good garment. Don't make the mistake of buying a cheap hunter orange vest as an afterthought. It will tear as soon as you walk through brush, and its noise will spook every elk within hearing distance.

If you ride to camp atop a horse, tie a warm jacket and raincoat on the saddle behind you. Better to be prepared than to thoroughly irritate the outfitter by asking him to unpack your duffle and retrieve a coat if it gets cold on the way to camp.

Don't be caught in this situation. Use logic when you head for elk country. A 4 wheel drive isn't the total answer, as demonstrated by premier Washington hunter, Dan Boes.

Ralph Stuart, Outdoor Life's Associate Editor (right) was well-prepared for this late Montana hunt. Despite temperatures of minus 10 below, and 50 mph winds, he took a good bull.

Personal Gear

This is one area where you want to be prepared. Bring a toilet kit that will store your medicines and personal items. It's a good idea to bring along aspirin, cough syrup, antibiotics, laxatives, antacid medication, diarrhea preventatives, effervescent tablets, and other items. If you take prescribed medication, be sure you have an adequate supply.

A small first-aid kit is handy for minor cuts and scrapes. If you're hunting with an outfitter, he should have one, but most hunters like to bring their own little emergency kit.

A flashlight is a must, not only to carry in your daypack, but to use in the tent. When the lantern goes out, you'll be depending on your flashlight to find your way in the dark.

Bring an empty pillow case and fill it with soft, clean clothes. It doubles as a real pillow, and works like a charm.

Alcohol is a personal preference. Use good sense when it comes to drinking. You came to hunt, and you want to be in top shape each day. If you hunt with an outfitter, you'll need to bring your own liquor. Very few outfitters provide it.

Hunt Gear

You'll need whatever equipment that's necessary to reduce a carcass to manageable sizes, as well as items for your daypack. A good pocketknife is always recommended, along with a sharpening stone. A compass is a must, along with waterproof matches, TWO small flashlights containing FRESH batteries, space blanket, fifty feet of nylon rope, maps of the area you're hunting, extra cartridges, candle, mirror, hard candy, meat saw, and trail food. Most items should fit in your daypack. To keep them dry, store them in Zip-Loc bags.

If you hunt with an outfitter, he should give you a checklist of equipment. Always pack gear in soft duffles rather than hard suitcases, and bring a soft case for your rifle.

Go over your gear list carefully before you leave home. The biggest mistake is packing too much rather than not enough. Just remember the words COLD and WET. Prepare for both and you'll be in good shape.

Appendix

State-by-State
Directory

Arizona

It's interesting that Arizona comes first in alphabetical order. Astute elk hunters know that Arizona has some of the biggest bulls in the West, and many are betting that the next world-record bull will come from this state. Arizona ranks extremely high for elk in the Boone and Crockett and Pope and Young record books.

Despite Arizona's popularity as a desert region, almost 7,000 square miles of elk habitat can be found here, and the Fort Apache and San Carlos Indian reservations contribute an enormous amount of elk country as well. About 80 percent of the elk habitat is on national forests. The bulk of the elk country is in the region from Flagstaff along the Mogollon rim to the New Mexico border.

The trend in elk harvest has been upward since 1968. Elk populations increased to their peak in recent years in the Flagstaff area, but they continue to increase in the White Mountains of eastern Arizona. Big bulls live everywhere in elk country.

Hunters must apply for elk tags in a lottery that has a late June application deadline. The regular elk hunt runs from late November to early December.

For information on hunting regulations, contact the Arizona Game and Fish Department, 2222 W. Greenway Road, Phoenix, AZ 85023 (602/942-3000).

National Forests:

Apache-Sitgreaves National Forest, Federal Bldg., P.O. Box
    640, Springerville, AZ (602)/333-4301).
Coconino National Forest, 2323 E. Greenlaw Lane, Flagstaff,
    AZ 86001 (602/779-3311).
Coronado National Forest, 301 W. Congress, P.O. Box 551,
    Tucson, AZ 85702 (602/792-6483).
Kaibab National Forest, 800 S. Sixth St., Williams, AZ 86046
    (602/635-2681).
Prescott National Forest, 344 S. Cortez, P.O. Box 2549,
    Prescott, AZ 86031 (602/445-1762).
Tonto National Forest, 102 S. 28th St., P.O. Box 29070,
    Phoenix, AZ 85038 (602/261-5205).

Bureau of Land Management: Arizona State Office, 2400
Valley Bank Center, Phoenix, AZ 85073 (602/261-3873).

Colorado

This is the top elk state in terms of populations, number
of elk hunters, and harvest. About 200,000 hunters take some
30,000 elk annually. Some 180,000 elk inhabit the state.

The world record bull was killed in Colorado before the
turn of the century, but the days of record-class bulls in
Colorado seem to be gone forever. However, a new quality
hunting program might turn this dismal picture around. Of
late, 20 units were set aside that restrict the number of
hunters. Quotas are set in each unit, and permits must be
obtained in a lottery.

Unlimited numbers of licenses and easy access to much of
Colorado's elk country is often blamed for the abundance of
small bulls and poor bull-to-cow ratio.

All of western Colorado is elk country, with the exception
of agricultural regions. Much of the area is national forest,
with plenty of public access.

Colorado offers three general hunts, all combined with
deer. Hunters can participate in only one season. A bull must
have at least four points on one side to be legal during many
hunts.

The early season has an advantage because elk are relatively undisturbed, except by bow and black-powder hunters.

The later hunt allows hunters a good opportunity if heavy snow drives elk out of the high country and into lower regions accessible to hunters.

For a big bull, your best chances are in the backcountry if you hunt during the general season. Good bulls are taken from most of Colorado's national forests, but some of the best hunting is on private land. Expect to find crowded conditions on public land where there is good access.

Practically every private ranch is leased in Colorado. It's very difficult to obtain hunting permission on private lands in prime elk country.

For information on hunting regulations, contact the Colorado Division of Wildlife, 6060 Broadway, Denver, CO 80216 (303/297-1192).

National Forests:

Arapaho and Roosevelt National Forests, Federal Bldg., 301 S. Howes, Fort Collins, CO 80521 (303/482-5155).

Grand Mesa, Uncompahgre, and Gunnison National Forests, 11th and Main St., P.O. Box 138, Delta, CO 81416 (303/874-7691).

Pike and San Isabel National Forests, 910 Highway 50 West, Pueblo, CO 81008 (303/544-5277).

Rio Grande National Forest, 1803 W. Highway 160, Monte Vista, CO 81144 (303/852-5941).

Routt National Forest, Hunt Bldg., Steamboat Springs, CO 80477 (303/879-1722).

San Juan National Forest, Federal Bldg., 701 Camino Del Rio, Durango, CO 81301 (303/247-4874).

White River National Forest, Old Federal Bldg., Box 948, Glenwood Springs, CO 81601 (303/945-6582).

Bureau of Land Management: Colorado State Office, Colorado State Bank Bldg., 1600 Broadway, Denver, CO 80202 (303/837-4325).

Idaho

A growing elk population is quickly putting Idaho back in the ranks with other top elk states. Hunters are taking an excess of 15,000 elk annually, and the prognosis for the future is bright. About 125,000 elk currently dwell in Idaho.

All of the state's mountainous regions have elk. National forests in the Panhandle and regions along and south of the Salmon River have good elk herds.

Several wilderness areas in Idaho offer excellent hunting. The Selway Wilderness, one of the biggest in North America, has some big bulls and offers an early general firearms season in some units.

The statewide general elk hunt starts in October, but dates vary with the units.

Idaho ranks high in the Boone and Crockett record book for record-class bulls and will likely produce more trophy heads in the future.

The Panhandle region has some thickly timbered forests, among the densest in the Rockies. Elk are tough to find in the heavy cover, but persistent hunters do well every year. Cows are often legal game in the Panhandle.

Resident tags are unlimited; nonresidents must obtain a license on a first-come basis. In recent years the nonresident quota has been selling out rapidly.

For information on hunting regulations, contact the Idaho Department of Fish and Game, 600 S. Walnut, P.O. Box 25, Boise, ID 83707 (208/334-3700).

National Forests:

Boise National Forest, 1075 Park Blvd., Boise, ID 83706 (208/334-1516).

Caribou National Forest, 250 S. Fourth Ave., Pocatello, ID 83201 (208/232-1142).

Challis National Forest, Forest Service Bldg., Challis, ID 83226 (208/879-2285).

Clearwater National Forest, Rt. 4, Orofino, ID 83544 (208/476-4541).

Idaho Panhandle National Forest, 1201 Ironwood Drive, Couer d'Alene, ID 83814 (208/667-2561).

Nez Perce National Forest, 319 E. Main St., Grangeville, ID 83530 (208/983-1950).

Payette National Forest, forest Service Bldg., P.O. Box 1026, McCall, ID 83638 (208/634-2255).

Salmon National Forest, Forest Service Bldg., Salmon, ID 83467 (208/756-2215).

Sawtooth National Forest, 1525 Addison Ave. East, Twin Falls, ID 83301 (208/733-3698).

Targhee National Forest, 420 N. Bridge St., St. Anthony, ID 83455 (208/624-3151).

Bureau of Land Management: Idaho State Office, 398 Federal Bldg., 550 W. Fort St., Boise, ID 83724 (208/384-1401).

Montana

The biggest of our Rocky Mountain states has a fine elk population, with an estimated 85,000 animals. Montana has the distinction of producing more Boone and Crockett trophy-class elk than any other state, with the 62 heads listed in the current edition of the book.

Western Montana's mountain ranges are home to the elk, although there are some excellent herds in isolated areas east of the mountains. The C.M. Russell Wildlife Refuge offers a fine hunt annually, but there is plenty of competition for the lottery-drawn permits.

Big bulls are killed everywhere in Montana's mountains, but some of the biggest are consistently taken from the Yellowstone Park region. Two units, the Gallatin and Gardiner, offer very late hunts that run from early December to late February. A lottery draw is required to obtain a tag. In both areas, elk migrating out of Yellowstone Park are hunted during the two- and four-day seasons.

Several national forests provide excellent hunting. The huge Bob Marshall Wilderness has plenty of elk, and the wilderness as well as areas adjacent to Yellowstone offer an early general gun season.

The statewide general season begins in late October and runs into late November, allowing five weeks of hunting.

Resident tags are unlimited, but nonresidents must buy

a tag on a first-come basis. The quota sells out quickly, as soon as the licenses go on sale. Nonresidents must purchase a combination elk license, which is also good for deer, black bear, birds, and fishing.

For information on hunting regulations, contact the Montana Division of Fish, Wildlife, and Parks, 1420 E. Sixth Ave., Helena, MT 59601 (406/444-2535).

National Forests:

Beaverhead National Forest, P.O. Box 1258, Dillon, MT 59725 (406/683-2312).

Bitterroot National Forest, 316 N. Third St., Hamilton, MT 59840 (406/363-3131).

Custer National Forest, P.O. Box 2556, Billings, MT 59103 (406/657-6361).

Deerlodge National Forest, Federal Bldg., P.O. Box 400, Butte, MT 59701 (406/723-6561).

Flathead National Forest, P.O Box 147, 290 N. Main, Kalispell, MT 59901 (406/755-5401).

Gallatin National Forest, Federal Bldg., P.O. Box 430, Bozeman, MT 59715 (406/587-5271).

Helena National Forest, Federal Bldg., Drawer 10014, Helena, MT 59601 (406/449-5201).

Kootenai National Forest, W. Highway 2, Libby, MT 59923 (406/293-6211).

Lewis and Clark National Forest, Federal Bldg., Great Falls, MT 59403 (406/453-7678.

Bureau of Land Management: Montana State Office, 222 N. 32nd St., P.O. Box 30157, Billings, MT 59107 (406/657-6462).

New Mexico

This southwest state has a healthy population of elk and annually gives up some very large bulls. This is the state that has the extensive private tracts that offer quality hunting to hunters who want a big bull without the pack-in backcountry-type trip. Those hunts are comparatively expensive, but hunter success is extremely high, often better than 90 percent on some ranches. These are wild elk, not fenced in animals that might be found in preserves.

About 35,000 elk live in New Mexico, with an annual harvest of abut 2,500 animals.

Besides the ranches, some Indian reservations have very good elk hunting, but prices are high as well. Some good bulls are killed on the tribal lands, with a very high hunter success rate.

National forests provide good elk hunting in New Mexico, especially in the northern half of the state. Part of the famous Vermejo Ranch was given to the U.S. Forest Service recently. It is now managed by the state wildlife department as a quality area.

Elk seasons vary with the unit, starting in October. Usually there are five different hunts, each less than one week long. A hunter may hunt only one season.

Tags for public land are issued in a lottery to residents and nonresidents alike. On private lands, landowners may distribute a quota of tags as they wish.

For information on hunting regulations, contact the New Mexico Game and Fish Department, Villagra Bldg., Sante Fe, NM 87503 (505/827-7899).

National Forests:

Carson National Forest, Forest Service Bldg., P.O. Box 558, Taos, NM 87571 (505/758-2238).

Cibola National Forest, 10308 Candelaria NE, Albuquerque, NM 87112 (505/766-2185).

Gila National Forest, 2610 N. Silver St., Silver City, NM 88061 (505/388-1986).

Lincoln National Forest, Federal Bldg., 11th and New York, Alamogordo, NM 88310 (505/437-6030).

Santa Fe National Forest, Federal Bldg., Box 1689, Sante Fe, NM 87501 (505/988-6328).

Bureau of Land Management: New Mexico State Office, Federal Bldg., South Federal Place, Sante Fe, NM 87501 (505/988-6217).

Oregon

Both subspecies of elk, the Roosevelt's and Rocky Mountain, live in Oregon. The Roosevelt's elk inhabits the Cascade Mountains west to the Coast Range, and Rocky Mountain elk occupy the region in eastern oregon. Officially, elk living west of Interstate 5 are Roosevelt's.

About 106,000 elk are estimated to live in Oregon, about 60 percent of them the Rocky Mountain subspecies.

Roosevelt's elk dwell in extremely dense rain forests. Hunting is done by watching openings from log decks or clearcut areas, or sneaking through the very heavy timber. Several national forests and private paper companies offer hunting opportunities in both western and eastern Oregon.

Trophy hunters should try the Snake River, Minam, and Imnaha units in the northeast for big bulls. There may be a minimum-size antler restriction in these quality areas.

On the west side, trophy hunters can try the Tioga Unit in the southwest and the Saddle Mountain Unit in the northwest. There are also minimum size antler restrictions in these units.

Oregon often ranks second only to Colorado in terms of numbers of elk harvested, with more than 20,000 usually taken each season. Most elk killed are the Rocky Mountain subspecies.

Elk tags are unrestricted for residents and nonresidents. Seasons for Rocky Mountain elk usually start in October; Roosevelt's elk seasons start in November.

For information on hunting regulations, contact the Oregon Department of Fish and Wildlife, P.O. Box 3503, Portland, OR 97208 (503/229-5551).

National Forests:

Deschutes National Forest, 211 NE Revere Ave., Bend, OR 97701 (503/382-6922).
Fremont National Forest, 34 North D St., Lakeview, OR 976320 (503/947-2151).
Malheur National Forest, 139 NE Dayton St., John Day, OR 97845 (503/575-1731).

Mt. Hood National Forest, 2440 SE 195th, Portland, OR 97233 (503/667-0511).

Ochoco National Forest, Federal Bldg., Prineville, OR 97754 (503/447-6247).

Rogue River National Forest, Federal Bldg., 333 W. Eighth St., P.O. Box 520, Medford, OR 97501 (503/779-2351).

Siskiyou National Forest, P.O. Box 440, Grants Pass, OR 97526 (503/479-5301).

Siuslaw National Forest, P.O. Box 1148, Corvallis, OR 97330 (503/757-4480).Umatilla National Forest, 2517 SW Halley Ave., Pendleton, OR 97801 (503/276-3811).

Umpqua National Forest, Federal Office Bldg., Roseburg, OR 97470 (503/672-6601).

Wallowa and Whitman National Forests, Federal Office Bldg., P.O. Box 907, Baker, OR 97814 (503/523-6391)

Willamette National Forest, 211 E. Seventh Ave., Eugene, OR 97440 (503/687-6533).

Winema National Forest, P.O. Box 1390, Klamath Falls, OR 97601 (503/882-7761).

Bureau of Land Management: 729 NE Oregon St., P.O. Box 2965, Portland, OR 97208 (503/234-4001).

Utah

Elk herds are scattered around Utah; most of them are in the north and northeast regions. A herd of about 45,000 lives in the state, with about 6,000 killed annually.

Utah has never produced an official record-class elk, but some good bulls are taken each year from scattered areas. The best hunting is in restricted units that require a lottery draw for a tag.

Transplanted herds in the south and central regions are growing rapidly and are giving up some nice bulls. One of the best is the Book Cliffs herd in the northeast. Hunters who draw a permit here have an excellent chance of taking a fine, mature bull.

The High Uintas Primitive Area in the northern region offers backcountry hunting to sportsmen who are prepared to penetrate this large, remote region.

Utah's biggest elk dwell on the Ute Indian reservations, but nontribal members have not been allowed to hunt it for years. If that changes, the area will likely produce a record-class head.

The general elk season starts in early October and runs for two weeks. The first part of the season coincides with the rut, but heavy pressure from hunters and plenty of easy access often stymie hunters who try to bugle bulls.

Permits are unrestricted but must be purchased prior to a late summer cutoff date.

For information on hunting regulations, contact the Utah Division of Wildlife Resources, 1596 W. North Temple, Salt Lake City, UT 84116 (801/533-9333).

National Forests:

Ashley National Forest, 437 E. Main St., Vernal, UT 84078 (801/789-1181).

Dixie National Forest, 82 N. 100 E. St., Cedar City, UT 84720 (801/586-2421).

Fishlake National Forest, 170 N. Main St., richfield, UT 84701 (801/896-4491).

Manti-Lasal National Forest, 599 West 100 South, Price, UT 84501 (801/637-2817).

Uinta National Forest, 88 West 1 North, Provo, UT 84601 (801/584-9101).

Wasatch National Forest, 8226 Federal Bldg., 125 S. State St., Salt Lake City, UT 84138 (801/524-5030).

Bureau of Land Management: Utah State Office, University Club Bldg., 136 South Temple, Salt Lake City, UT 84111 (801/524-5311).

Washington

This state has areas of very heavy timber and has an excellent and thriving elk population. The Rosevelt's subspecies occupies the forests of the Cascade Mountains west to the Coast forests. The Rocky Mountain elk lives in the eastern regions, in mountain ranges that have very good elk habitat.

National forests provide plenty of good public hunting in both regions, and a wealth of private paper companies allow hunting on much of their lands.

The Rocky Mountain subspecies is the most popular in Washington, perhaps because it lives in more open landscape and has larger antlers. Roosevelt's elk are bigger in body stature, but they're extremely difficult to hunt in the dense western forests.

About 60,000 elk live in Washington, with about 35,000 being the Roosevelt's subspecies and 25,000 the Rocky Mountain subspecies. The average annual harvest for both species runs about 10,000.

Season dates vary, depending on the region, and there are some excellent quality units with varying dates as well. The quality areas offer a superb opportunity for a nice bull, and hunter success rates are much higher than the statewide average.

Licenses are unlimited to residents and nonresidents.

For information on hunting regulations, contact the Washington Game Department, 600 N. Capitol Way, Olympia, WA 98504 (206/753-5700).

National Forests:

Colville National Forest, Colville, WA 99114 (509/684-5221).

Gifford Pinchot National Forest, 500 W. 12th St., Vancouver, WA 98660 (206/696-4041).

Mt. Baker and Snoqualmie National Forests, 1601 Second Ave., Seattle, WA 98101 (206/442-5400).

Okanogan National Forest, 1240 Second Ave. S., Okanogan, WA 98840 (509/422-2704).

Olympia National Forest, P.O. Box 2288, Olympia, WA 98507 (206/753-9534).

Wenatchee National Forest, 301 Yakima St., Wenatchee, WA 98801 (509/662-4823).

Bureau of Land Management: 729 NE Oregon St., P.O. Box 2965, Portland, OR 97208 (503/234-4001).

Wyoming

Most elk populations are in the western mountains of Wyoming, with large concentrations in Yellowstone National Park, Teton National Park, and adjacent national forests. The Shoshone and Bridger-Teton National forests are popular areas for elk in the western region. In the south-central area, the Medicine Bow National Forest has good elk hunting. The Bighorn National Forest in the North-central region is well known for elk.

A unique elk hunt is held in the Red Desert each year. Hunters seek elk in low elevations, most of it sagebrush and prairie. This and other quality hunts like it offer elk hunting to sportsmen who win tags in a lottery. Special late hunts are held annually in Teton National Park and the National Elk Refuge.

Wyoming's biggest elk come from scattered locations, but the Wyoming Range in the Bridger-Teton National Park is one of the best spots. The Shoshone National Forest east of Yellowstone Park is also a fine spot for big bulls.

Elk season normally begins October 1 or 15, depending on the unit, but dates vary in others. Some early backcountry hunts are held in September. They occur during the rut and are superb hunts for taking big bulls.

Residents obtain general licenses on an unlimited basis; nonresidents must apply for a tag each year with an application deadline of February 1. About 7,000 tags are available to nonresidents.

During a typical year, 55,000 hunters pursue elk, with an annual harvest of about 20,000. Wyoming's elk herd numbers about 80,000 animals.

For information on hunting regulations, write the Wyoming Game and Fish Department, Cheyenne, WY 82002.

National Forests:

Bridger-Teton National Forest, Forest Service Bldg., Jackson, Wy 83001 (307/733-2752).
Bighorn National Forest, Columbus Bldg., P.O. Box 2046, Sheridan, WY 82801 (307/672-2457).

Medicine Bow National Forest, 605 Skyline Drive, Laramie,
WY 82070 (307/745-8971).
Shoshone National Forest, West Yellowstone Highway, P.O.
Box 2140, Cody, WY 82414 (307/587-2274

Bureau of Land Management: Wyoming State Office, 2515
Warren Ave., P.O. Box 1828, Cheyenne, WY 82001 (307/778-
2326).

Alberta

There is a fine elk herd in this Canadian province,
including some enormous bulls. It is interesting to note that
the biggest elk of the 20th century was killed in Alberta in
1977.

Alberta once had an elk population of about 30,000
animals, but excessive crop damage and competition with
livestock led to a reduction in the mid-1960's and early 1970's.
Currently, a healthy herd of about 13,000 exists. Hunters
harvest about 2,000 elk annually.

Elk are found in four major habitat types. They include
subalpine, boreal mixed woods, boreal uplands, and boreal
foothills.

For information on hunting regulations, contact the
Alberta Fish and Wildlife Division, Petroleum Plaza Bldg.,
Edmonton, Alberta, Canada, T5H 2C9 (403/427-6749).

British Columbia

There is a healthy population of about 35,000 elk in
British Columbia. The harvest runs about 3,000 annually, and
some excellent bulls are killed.

Roosevelt's elk occur on Vancouver Island and
occasionally find their way to the lower mainland from
Washington State. Rocky Mountain elk occur mainly in the
Kootenays (the Rocky, Purcell, Selkirk, and Monashee
mountain ranges) and farther north (Omineca-Peace Resource
Management Region) in lower Peace River area (the Murray-
Wapiti River drainages) and the Muskwa-Prophet River
drainages on the eastern slope of the Rocky Mountains.

For information on hunting regulations, contact the British Columbia Fish and Wildlife Branch, Parliament Bldgs., Victoria, British Columbia, Canada V8V 1X4 (604/387-6409).

Jim Zumbo's
<u>Elk Memories</u>
A Photo Album

My horse, Silver, now deceased,
packs my elk out of the
hills. He was a great hunting
horse. <u>Colorado, 1982</u>

Hal Mechom is a trusting
soul — using a horse as a
stepladder is a bad idea!
Don't try this unless you have
a high pain threshold and
your medical insurance is
adequate — Colorado 1982

Murry Burnham, one of my
favorite hunting pals, bugles
into an aspen patch. Murry
imitates animal sounds better
than anyone else I know. Colorado 1981

One of the nice things about
getting your bull is the
ability to do other things
in the high country —
like fish and sleep —

British Columbia 1987

Four big bulls, all taken in
Alberta. Pat Bates, second from
left, is a tough Canadian
outfitter who really knows
his stuff! Alberta, 1986

Spencer Kugler, 12, with a dandy
six point bull. How many
grown men would like to
take such a fine elk!

Montana 1985

Elk camp is more than just
hunting — we were well-entertained
in Wyoming's Gros Ventre Range!
                    Wyoming 83

A big part of elk hunting is
being with good friends — and
recalling those memories years
later. Washington, 1988

We looked the World Record
Plute elk and took it up
the mountain to photograph it.
Was I nervous with that rack
bouncing around or what!
Colorado, 1985

I've ridden to elk camp every way
imaginable, but this was original!
Alberta, 1986

I use one of the old-time
bugle calls. It worked then,
and it still works now.
Utah 1976

Billy Stockton is the sawiest
elk outfitter I know! I say
that because with his assistance
I managed to down a bull
with a bow! I was impressed.

Montana, 1984

My favorite horse scene in one
of my favorite places — Idaho's
Selway Wilderness. Idaho 1983

This, in my opinion, is the
very best way to transport an
elk! Funny thing — almost
everyone else agrees! New Mexico 1981

This bull fell in the nastiest
spot in the Selway. It took
us 2½ days to get him
out — Idaho, 1984

The European Red Stag is classified
exactly the same as our elk.
They're biologically the same animal.
I pose with my stag after
an interesting hunt — Spain, 1985

Chuck Yeager taught me a beautiful
European custom — we gave my bull
its last bite. A real touch of
class, and I thank Chuck for
his insights   British Columbia 1987

The nice thing about being a
writer / photographer / hunter is that
you always have an excuse to
get out of the dirty work.
Photos are priority! Colorado 1982

I'm signing the contract for
my HUNT ELK book. Bob
Elman, editor with Winchester
Press, looks on. What better
place than to sign for an elk
book than elk camp? Wyoming 1983

Elk habitat isn't always in
the boonies — Gardiner, Montana 1985

BOOKS and VIDEOS by JIM ZUMBO

BOOKS

All books will be autographed

CALLING ALL ELK — Brand new, the only book on the subject of elk hunting that covers every aspect of elk vocalization. $17.95 postpaid.

JIM ZUMBO'S GUIDE TO MODERN MULE DEER HUNTING — A jam-packed softcover that will lead you to big muleys. Foreward by Pat McManus. Lots of photos, tips, secrets, techniques, where-to, how-to. $11.95 postpaid.

HUNT ELK — The most comprehensive book ever written on elk hunting. This 260-page hardcover describes everything you've ever wanted to know about elk — bugling, hunting in timber, late season hunting, trophy hunting, solid advice on hunting on your own or with an outfitter, and lots more. $20.95 postpaid.

HUNTING AMERICA'S MULE DEER — The first book ever done on every phase of mule deer hunting. This thick 360-page hardcover is acclaimed to be the best on the subject. Plenty of photos, with valuable information on trophy hunting and where-to, and how-to hunt muley bucks. $20.95 postpaid.

HOW TO PLAN YOUR WESTERN BIG GAME HUNT — Are you dreaming of a western hunt? This softcover will start you in the right direction, with solid info on planning your hunt. Lots of maps and phone numbers, and precise info on all western big game species. $11.95 postpaid.

ALL AMERICAN DEER HUNTER'S GUIDE — A big, 340-page hardcover with color photos that covers every aspect of hunting whitetails and muleys. Co-edited by Jim Zumbo and Robert Elman. Chapters by other experts such as Jim Carmichel, Craig Boddington, Erwin Bauer, Leonard Lee Rue, Byron Dalrymple, and many others. $32.95 postpaid.

VIDEOS

HUNTING BUGLING ELK WITH JIM ZUMBO — produced by Sportsmen On Film — 70 minutes. Watch Jim fly in to Idaho's Selway Wilderness and hunt elk. This video is loaded with instructions and tips on elk bugling, and is climaxed by Jim taking a big 6-point bull on camera. $29.95 postpaid.

LATE SEASON ELK WITH JIM ZUMBO — produced by Sportsmen On Film — 38 minutes. See huge elk plowing through deep powder snow, and watch a 12-year old boy take a big bull on camera. Lots of tips and techniques included. $29.95 postpaid.

HUNTING AMERICA'S MULE DEER — produced by 3M Corp. — 60 minutes. Acclaimed to be the best mule deer video ever produced. Watch Jim stalk and kill a nice four-point buck. Plenty of specific info on techniques. Filmed in Wyoming. $52.95 postpaid.

(continued next page...)

VIDEOS *(cont'd)*

HUNTING BIGHORN SHEEP WITH JIM ZUMBO — produced by Grunkmeyer Productions — 60 minutes. Watch Jim stalk and shoot a ram in Wyoming's spectacular Teton Wilderness with veteran outfitter Nate Vance. $52.95 postpaid.

AUDIO CASSETTES

E-Z ELK CALL INSTRUCTIONAL TAPE — 30 minutes. Jim Zumbo tells where, how and when to use the E-Z Elk Call, including hunt scenarios and situations. $12.95 postpaid.

HOW TO HUNT ELK IN CROWDED WOODS — 30 minutes. Jim Explains how to beat the odds where competition from other hunters is heavy. $12.95 postpaid.

HOW AND WHERE TO HUNT TROPHY BULLS. Jim describes successful methods for hunting mature elk as well as specific where-to-go info in each elk state and Canadian province. 60 minutes. $15.95 postpaid.

E-Z ELK CALL

JIM ZUMBO'S E-Z ELK CALL. Made of very soft plastic, both calling edges are of different lengths, allow calls of varying pitches. $12.95 postpaid.

Order from

JIM ZUMBO
P.O. Box 2390
Cody, WY 82414

Check, money order or Visa/MC accepted. Credit card orders: please include number and expiration date. Allow 6 weeks for delivery. Canadian residents add $2.00 for each item for shipping.